The Women of
1916

When History Was Made...

The Women of
1916

Ruth Taillon

First published in 1996
by
Beyond the Pale Publications
PO Box 337
Belfast BT9 7BT
Tel: +44 (0)1232 645930

British Library Cataloguing-in-Publication Data.
A catalogue record for this book is available from the British Library.

ISBN 0 9514229 8 7

Typeset in 10 on 13pt Times
Printed by
Colour Books Ltd, Dublin

Cover photograph: Molly Childers and Mary Spring-Rice on board the Asgard, bringing guns into Howth, Co. Dublin, July 1914.

CONTENTS

Acknowledgements

A few people, in particular, helped to make this book a reality. I would like to thank especially Liz Curtis and Penny Duggan for their enthusiasm, encouragement and many contributions of valuable information; Pat Harper for taking on the daunting task of reading the draft manuscript and offering a number of useful suggestions; and the Mary Ann McCracken Historical Society for their support and inspiration.

Invisible Women

The singer sings a rebel song
and everybody sings along.
Just one thing I'll never understand:
Every damn rebel seems to be a man.

For he sings of the Bold Fenian Men
And the Boys of the Old Brigade.
What about the women who stood there too
"When history was made" ...?

Ireland, Mother Ireland, with your freedom-loving sons,
Did your daughters run and hide at the sound of guns?
Or did they have some part in the fight
And why does everybody try to keep them out of sight?

For they sing of the Men of the West
And the Boys of Wexford too.
Were there no women living round those parts;
Tell me, what did they do ...?

BRIAN MOORE

Foreword

This book has been a long time waiting to be written — eighty years, in fact. It is a sad thought, particularly since, as I write, I am made aware of the recent death in Seattle of Lily Kempson, at 99 years of age. Did ever a nation treat its founders with more contempt?

When the 19-year-old Lily Kempson was making her final preparations for the Rising, my maternal grandmother was behind the bar of her husband's public house, in Cookstown, Co. Tyrone, preparing the parting glass for the men in her kitchen. That the Volunteers for the Rising assembled there to await the Dublin train was information I possessed since childhood. I was also told of the confusion caused in the company by the arrival of the newspaper countermanding the mobilisation for the Rising and that consequently a determined few took the train, leaving behind enough men to play a proper game of football in the big yard before dispersing.

Jimmy Tomney was one of those who took the train. Many years later, he took time to offer unsolicited advice to a young woman 'civil-righter' on first meeting — 'Stick with the extremists, girl' — and to recall fondly that my grandmother was the finest woman on Slieve Gallon's braes. Sadly, Jimmy was dead when the story, attributed to him, of the part played by John Ban's wife, my grandmother, was recalled. It seemed

x

that she had been dispatched by her husband, twenty years her senior, to bring drinks for the volunteers. In her absence the newspaper arrived, and by her return the debate was under way. She was instructed to serve first the men with a train to catch, which she did. Then, she walked to the scullery, without a word, poured the remainder away and left the company.

There is no way of checking the accuracy of the story. No other evidence of Mary Jane expressing a political view exists. At the time of its telling all who were party to the reality were dead. It remains, however, a thread across time waiting to be traced through its invisible course to the present. Could the small band in her kitchen have ever believed what the future held? Young Tomney would survive to strike again for freedom more than sixty years later. John Ban and Mary Jane would have a daughter whose daughter would give England a run for its money. And John Ban's brother would produce a grandson to lie in the H-blocks on hunger strike for his dignity and political recognition.

In 1916 Dublin, living to be 99 years of age and dying in America had to be the least likely thought in the mind of Lily Kempson. Of the little lives of little people is history made, and forgotten, until the invisible thread is woven into view again.

In producing *The Women of 1916* Ruth Taillon has not only rescued the past; she has not merely put the women in the picture of the GPO but also broadened and deepened our thinking about Easter Week. She has also, I believe, created a new space for women and inspired a new interest in researching and documenting women's involvement, in all its diversity, both past and present. This is work which has not yet been done and it should not be confused with ideological argument about what others *thought* women were doing or should have been doing.

Of Irish Protestant stock on her mother's side and French-Canadian, through her father, Ruth was born and raised in Canada, and, like most young North Americans in the late 1960s and early 1970s, she cut her political teeth and learned her political practice in the Vietnam anti-war movement. She developed her analysis and theory in the socialist movement.

On the principle of digging where you stand, she was also involved in the Quebec solidarity and fledgling feminist movements.

She left Canada in 1978, arriving in Ireland in early 1980, via Paris and London, just as the prison protests were about to explode. Again on the basis of digging where you stand, Ruth became active in progressive and feminist politics, which is where our separate streams joined the same river.

Ruth is currently Director of the West Belfast Economic Forum. A feminist, a socialist, but above all a practitioner, an activist. She is a founder member of the Mary Anne McCracken Historical Society.

Ruth brings to the historical research on the women of 1916 that living sense of shared sisterhood borne of common struggle. She writes of the sisters of the past with a sense of respect and familiarity that comes from the continuity of struggle, which is much, so much more than simply hanging on to your guns. You cannot but be moved to tears for Winifred Carney as the surrender progresses — not tears of pity, but of shared pain.

This is a powerful, empowering and honest book, and worth waiting for. Lily Kempson was 19 years old when she took part in the Easter Rising of 1916. If she had survived a few months longer, she would have lived to see her contribution finally acknowledged. She would have liked that.

Bernadette McAliskey
Coalisland, February 1996

Introduction

The Easter Rising of 1916, involving at most a few thousand active insurgents, was crushed in less than a week by the superior military might of the British forces. Nevertheless, it was to be one of the defining events in Irish history, an event which would ultimately lead to the foundation of the modern Irish state. Independent and united, Ireland could have become an icon to emerging nations around the world. The democratic and in many cases socialist, ideas of the men and women who fought in the Rising laid the foundations for the establishment of the 1st and 2nd Dáils. Their defeat in the Civil War of 1922-1923 left the field open for the carnival of reaction predicted by James Connolly. Intellectual, political and cultural life was decimated. Following the Civil War, many of the brightest and best were dead, imprisoned or had emigrated; those remaining were marginalised and demoralised. The island of Ireland was partitioned into two backward and confessional states. National independence has still not been achieved and many of the issues which faced the Irish people in 1916 remain unresolved eight decades on. It is, therefore, worth re-examining the experience of early republicanism to see what lessons there are for those striving to achieve democracy in Ireland today.

Over the intervening years, much of the historical and political analysis of the Rising has been reduced to a sterile debate between on the one hand, those who have elevated the 1916 leaders to mythic status and the 'revisionists' who have used historical discourse as a means to attack modern day republicanism. In both cases the result has often been to create a caricature of the 1916 rebels — a cult of heroes and martyrs to be celebrated or derided according to one's political viewpoint. Likewise, where the participation of women in the Rising has been acknowledged, it too has been largely reduced to caricature and stereotype.

It cannot be argued that the information required to give a more balanced perspective has not been available. There are numerous personal accounts written by women about their involvement in Easter Week of which the historians have been aware. That knowledge has not prevented these historians relegating the women of the Rising to the margins of the story. Desmond Ryan's authoritative account, *The Rising* (ironically sub-titled 'The Complete Story of Easter Week'), is one example. The index of Ryan's book contains a total of only 43 citations referring to individual women or the organisation Cumann na mBan. Three of these are merely footnotes; no less than 12 others are references to books or articles written by women cited in footnotes. (Indeed, seven of these are contained in one footnote: "The part played by the Cumann na mBan in Easter Week is dealt with in articles by ..."[1]). He himself manages to sum up the involvement of women in a single paragraph:

> ... Pearse regarded the activities of the women in Easter Week with intense admiration. It was due to his influence as much as MacDonagh's and Connolly's that the Proclamation formally recognised the right of woman's suffrage in a free Ireland. Until almost the end the Cumann na mBan shared the dangers, the fire, the bullets, all the ordeals of the fighters, in the most dangerous areas, on the barricades, through the bullet-swept streets and quay-sides, carrying dispatches, explosives, and ammunition through the thick of the fray, assisting in the hospital, cooking, and in some cases, approaching the British military posts to deliver warnings from Pearse

that the Red Cross posts of the insurgents had been fired on by British snipers while in the end it was a woman who marched out to initiate the final negotiations. So Winifred Carney's sharp retort to Pearse when he suggested she should leave the G.P.O. was somewhat mistaken.[2]

Mary MacSwiney is mentioned by Ryan twice in the text — in one case to quote an article written by her in 1922 and in another quoting her testimony to an American commission in 1920. In addition, Lady Maxwell is mentioned once — as the recipient of a letter from her husband. There is one reference to Áine Ceannt — "Ceannt returned home and told his wife the news..."[3] — and Winifred Carney is mentioned six times: on three occasions she is described as James Connolly's secretary, on another she is "weeping". Hanna Sheehy-Skeffington gets one sentence, in which she "reproached her husband for taking such a great risk".[4] Constance Markievicz is afforded a total of five sentences in the entire book, all of which cast her in an unflattering light. The following passage is the most overtly critical:

> Madame Markievicz was urging action on the Citizen Army, and it needed great nerve and patience to avoid her precipitate counsels and incitements, which he [Michael Mallin] was very well aware could not be carried out except at the risk of suicide, while the blunt warning he received in the course of his meeting with the Military Council showed him that the Volunteer organisation could not be dragged into action in these circumstances, as the leaders of the militant party which controlled them had warned him they would then be as hostile to action as the more moderate MacNeill group obviously would be. In his difficult game of calming the Citizen Army, controlling Madame Markievicz and her backers, and daring the Military Council, Mallin played a bad hand with skill.[5]

Elizabeth O'Farrell is treated more fairly. She is allocated a passage which runs to one and a half pages; but it would be difficult to exclude her from the story of the surrender.

The shabby treatment by historians of the 1916 women is one reason this book is necessary. This account, however, is intended to do more than fill a gap in Irish and feminist historiography. It will, first of all, acknowledge the women's contribution to a crucial event in the nation's history, restoring them to their rightful place in the story. Just as importantly, by including women's experiences and allowing them to interpret these experiences through their own words, it is possible to tell the story of Easter week fully, not partially, and in doing so, to reconsider the social and political significance of events.

In this context a new assessment of the part played by women in 1916 has a practical and not just a moral value. Women's social and political activism is not a new phenomenon in Ireland. Then, as in more recent times, women were centrally involved in every sphere of activity; but the importance of their contribution was rarely acknowledged. Today, among nationalist and republican men, some token gestures are made towards recognising women's involvement. We often hear that the struggle could not go on without the 'support' of women, or that women are 'the backbone' of the struggle. It is rarely spelt out what this means, and so we are left with the impression that women are only offering support to the 'main' struggle which is, by implication, being waged by men. Then, as today, women constituted much of the infrastructure on which the nationalist and democratic movements were built; without that infrastructure, those movements could not have existed.

The women who came out in Easter Week were not just 'supporting' the men in pursuit of generalised 'national' ideals which only included them by default. They were also asserting their claim to be part of the shaping of the nation and a share in determining the sort of society that would come. It was not just because of Pearse's or MacDonagh's or James Connolly's progressive views on women that the Proclamation of the Republic included universal suffrage and equality for all Irish citizens. The Proclamation reflected the very real influence and involvement of women in the national and labour movements of the time:

THE PROCLAMATION OF
POBLACHT NA hEIREANN

THE PROVISIONAL GOVERNMENT
OF THE
IRISH REPUBLIC
TO THE PEOPLE OF IRELAND

IRISHMEN AND IRISHWOMEN: In the name of God and of the dead generations from which she receives her old tradition of nationhood, Ireland, through us, summons her children to her flag and strikes for her freedom. [...]

We declare the right of the people of Ireland to the ownership of Ireland, and to the unfettered control of Irish destinies, to be sovereign and indefeasible. The long usurpation of that right by a foreign people and government has not extinguished the right, nor can it ever be extinguished except by the destruction of the Irish people. [...]

The Irish Republic is entitled to, and hereby claims, the allegiance of every Irishman and Irishwoman. The Republic guarantees religious and civil liberty, equal rights and equal opportunities to all its citizens, and declares its resolve to pursue the happiness and prosperity of the whole nation and of all its parts, cherishing all the children of the nation equally, and oblivious of the differences carefully fostered by an alien government, which have divided a minority from the majority in the past.

Until our arms have brought the opportune moment for the establishment of a permanent National Government, representative of the whole people of Ireland and elected by the suffrage of all her men and women, the Provisional Government, hereby constituted, will administer the civil and military affairs of the Republic in trust for the people.

[...]

Many of the women of 1916 considered themselves combatants, not mere auxiliaries, in the insurrection. As will be seen, many women were prepared to ignore the protestations of their male comrades and face whatever the consequences might be when they surrendered, as combatants, when the fighting was over. The men who were involved in the movement often had a very different perspective.

It has become an accepted assumption that the members of the Irish Citizen Army were more politically aware or socially progressive, especially on matters related to women's status, than were their comrades in the Volunteers and Cumann na mBan. The reality was more complex, however. It is true that there was no formal distinction between the status of male and female members of the ICA and indeed there were a number of women officers. However, most of the women were in the Ambulance Corps, which at least some ICA members later referred to as the 'Women's Section'. Cumann na mBan branches, on the other hand, were 'attached' to particular sections of the Volunteers, and there is no doubt that the male commanders were in overall charge. At the same time, however, the Cumann na mBan members maintained their own command structures and insisted on their right to take decisions about their own actions when the occasion required it.

It is likely that the women in both organisations were, in practice, subordinate to their male colleagues. That is the case for many women in similar positions today, who have the benefit of several decades of feminist theory and experience to inform them. Perhaps we should hesitate before being too critical of the choices made in 1916, or of applying standards of modern day political correctness to their actions, and instead give credit for having achieved the independence of action to the extent which they did.

Finally, it is necessary to say something about the naming of names in this book. The list of participants was put together from a number of sources, in particular the official list of prisoners, printed in the *Sinn Féin Rebellion Handbook*, published by the *Irish Times* in 1917; the official list of ICA members who participated in the Rising, contained in R.M. Fox's book *The Irish Citizen Army*; and a group photograph of 1916 veterans taken at a meeting of Irish National Aid Association in 1917, published in the *Irish Press* in 1966. Other names were garnered from various published accounts, all of which are listed in the bibliography.

Individual women have been named wherever possible — partly to give them the recognition they deserve and partly to allow for others to take up individual stories where further information might be available. Another reason, perhaps more important, was to compensate for the many general accounts of the Rising which have mentioned the women involved only in passing, or have grouped them together in a way which diminished their contributions, both individual and collective. It is not a complete list, and there are some instances in which there is some confusion about the spelling of an individual's name. It is also possible that there have been mistakes made in identifying women by both their birth name and their married names, or because they in different circumstances used both Irish and English versions of their names; Éilis, Elizabeth, Nell, Lizzie, or Betsy could all be the same person. While every effort has been made to be accurate, it is possible that some mistakes have been made. If any individual has been counted more than once, however, there is no doubt that there are several of her political sisters who have remained entirely anonymous. Where possible, a woman is called by her own forename and the name by which she was known at the time of the Rising. If she subsequently married, her married name, where known, is given also; but every attempt was made to avoid defining any woman simply by her husband's name. Too often in the past the independent contribution of nationalist women has been lost because they have been treated simply as the wives of male heroes.

It is time each and every one of them emerged from the footnotes of history.

Women in the 1916 Rising

Below is a list of names of all the women known to have taken part in the Easter Rising, together with a brief mention of what is known of their involvement. Because of gaps and discrepancies in the numerous accounts of the Rising, it has been impossible to be definitive. The full names of some of the women are unknown. On occasion, similar names may in fact relate to the same person. A few names are included of women whose involvement in the Rising is not proven beyond doubt. Finally, there are many other women who were involved whose names are not given here. The author would be most grateful for further names and information.

'Prisoner' indicates that the person was on the official list of internees, although others, such as Annie Higgins and Mary MacSwiney, were also arrested and held for various lengths of time.

Miss Adrian, Ashbourne
Lizzie Allen

Katie Barrett (formerly Connolly), City Hall; Prisoner
Bridget Brady, City Hall; Prisoner
Una Brennan (formerly Bolgar), Enniscorthy
Kate Brown (unclear whether she was mobilised in Dublin or
    Enniscorthy)
Martha Brown; Prisoner
Eileen Byrne; Prisoner
Katie Byrne; Prisoner
Mary (May) Byrne, Marrowbone; Prisoner

Chris Caffrey (Mrs. Keely), St. Stephen's Green
Winifred Carney, GPO; Prisoner, interned until Dec 1916
Máire (May) Carron (or McCarron), Four Courts and Father
    Mathew Hall; Prisoner
Alice Cashel, Cork
Maeve Cavanagh
Kathleen Clarke (formerly Daly); Prisoner
Kathleen Cleary, St. Stephen's Green
G. Colley
Gretta Comerford, Enniscorthy
Mrs. (Martin) Conlon, Father Mathew Hall
Ina Connolly
Nora Connolly
Annie Cooney; Prisoner
E. (Lily) Cooney; Prisoner
Marcella Cosgrove; Prisoner
Mary Cullen, GPO

Agnes Daly
Laura Daly (later Mrs. O'Sullivan)
Madge Daly, Limerick
Nora Daly (later Mrs. Eamonn Dore)
Bridget Davis (Mrs. Duffy), City Hall; Prisoner
Maggie Derham, Four Courts
Mary Devereux (Mrs. Allen), St. Stephen's Green
Bríd Dixon
Helen Donnelly
Kathy Doran
Frances Downey
Peggy Downey (later Mrs. Viant), GPO

Éilis Elliott, Father Mathew Hall
Emily Elliott, (later Mrs. Ledwith), Father Mathew Hall
M. Elliott
Ellen (Nellie) Ennis, Four Courts; Prisoner

Mrs. (Frank) Fahy, Father Mathew Hall
Bridie Farrell
Kathleen Fleming; Prisoner
Brigid Foley; Prisoner, interned until July 1916

Nora Foley (later Mrs. O'Daly) St. Stephen's Green; Prisoner
Miss Foley
Madeleine ffrench-Mullen

May Gahan, Imperial Hotel; Prisoner
Louise Gavan Duffy; GPO
Nell Gifford (later Mrs. Donnelly), St. Stephen's Green
Bridget Gough (Goff), St. Stephen's Green; Prisoner
Bridget Grace (GPO)
Éilis (Betsy) Gray
Julia Grenan, GPO; Prisoner
Mrs. (Arthur) Griffiths; Prisoner (Uncertain whether she took
    active part in Rising.)

Rosanna (Rosie) Hackett, St. Stephen's Green; Prisoner
Dora Harford, Father Mathew Hall
Christina Hayes, Father Mathew Hall
Bridget Hegarty; Prisoner
Annie Higgins, Hibernian Bank, GPO
P. Hoey
Ellen Humphreys; Prisoner
Mary (Molly) Hyland (Mrs. Kelly), St. Stephen's Green

Maggie Joyce, St. Stephen's Green; Prisoner

Sara Kealy, Jacob's
Kathleen Kearney (later Mrs. Behan)
Linda Kearns, North Great Georges St
Annie Kelly, St. Stephen's Green
Josephine Kelly; Prisoner
Kate (Kitty) Kelly, St. Stephen's Green; Prisoner
Martha Kelly; Prisoner
Lily Kempson, St. Stephen's Green
K. Kennedy
Margaret L. Kennedy, Marrowbone; Prisoner
Bridy Kenny; Prisoner
Kathleen Kenny, Father Mathew Hall

Kathleen Lane, Jacob's
Mrs. Lawless
Catherine Liston; Prisoner
Mary Liston; Prisoner
Bessie Lynch (Mrs. Kelly), City Hall; Prisoner
Dr Kathleen Lynn, City Hall; Prisoner
Brighid (Brigid) Lyons (later Dr Thornton), Four Courts; Prisoner

Julia McAley; Prisoner
Josephine McGowan; Prisoner
Katy McGuinness, Father Mathew Hall and Four Courts
Rose McGuinness, Four Courts
Maggie McLaughlin; Prisoner
Anastasia MacLoughlin
May MacLoughlin
Sorca McMahon
Agnes McNamara; Prisoner
Rose McNamara, Marrowbone; Prisoner
Agnes McNanice; Prisoner
Annie McQuade, Jacob's
Annie MacSwiney, Cork
Mary MacSwiney, Cork
Kathleen Maher; Prisoner
Pauline Markham; Prisoner
Constance Markievicz, St. Stephen's Green; Prisoner, sentenced
    to life imprisonment, released June 1917
Kathleen (Kate) Martin, Father Mathew Hall; Prisoner
Margaret Martin, Father Mathew Hall
Florence (Flossie) Mead, Four Courts; Prisoner
J. Milner
Caroline (Carrie) Mitchell, Four Courts; Prisoner
Helena Molony, City Hall; Prisoner, interned until December 1916
May Moore, St. Stephen's Green
P. Morecambe
Pauline Morkan, Four Courts
Mrs. Morkan, Four Courts
Lizzie Mulhall; Prisoner
Rose Mullally; Prisoner
Kathleen Murphy; Prisoner

Kathleen Murphy (from Belfast)
Rose Ann Murphy (later Mrs. (Henry) Morgan)
Mrs. (Seamus) Murphy, Father Mathew Hall
Lily Murnane, Father Mathew Hall
May Murray
Bridget Murtagh, St. Stephen's Green; Prisoner

Éilis Ní Chorra
Kathleen Ní Chorra
Áine Ní Rian, Reis's Chambers and Father Mathew Hall
Éilis Ní Rian (later Mrs. Sean O'Connell), Reis's Chambers and
    Father Mathew Hall
Máire Nic Shiubhlaigh (Molly Walker) (later Mrs. (Eamonn)
    Price), Jacob's
Mrs. Norgrove, St. Stephen's Green
Annie Norgrove (Mrs. Grange), City Hall; Prisoner
Emily Norgrove (Mrs. Hanratty), City Hall; Prisoner

Lily O'Brennan, Marrowbone; Prisoner
Éilis O'Connell, Four Courts
Katie O'Connor
Elizabeth O'Farrell, GPO
Margaret O'Flaherty; Prisoner
Sheila O'Hanlon; Prisoner
Eileen (Eily) O'Hanrahan (later Mrs. O'Hanrahan O'Reilly)
M. O'Hanrahan
Eileen O'Hegarty, Enniscorthy
Emily O'Keeffe; Prisoner
Josephine O'Keeffe; Prisoner
Mary O'Moore; Prisoner
Maura O'Neill Mackay, Four Courts
Miss O'Neill (from Belfast)
Miss O'Rahilly
Molly O'Reilly (later Mrs. Corcoran), City Hall
Dolly O'Sullivan, Four Courts
Grace O'Sullivan
Louisa O'Sullivan; Prisoner
Mollie O'Sullivan, Four Courts; Prisoner

Eileen Parker, Father Mathew Hall
Mary Partridge; Prisoner
Marie Perolz; Prisoner, interned until July 1916
Josie Pollard, Jacob's
Miss Pollard (sister of Josie), Jacob's
Leslie Price (later Mrs. Tom Barry), GPO
Maria Quigley; Prisoner
Priscilla Quigley; Prisoner
S. Quigley

Barbara Retz; Prisoner
Molly Reynolds, GPO
Agnes Ryan
K. Ryan
Máire (Mary or Min) Ryan, (later Mrs. Richard Mulcahy), GPO
Margaret Ryan (Mrs. Dunne), St. Stephen's Green
Nell Ryan; Prisoner, interned until December 1916
Phylis Ryan (later Mrs. O'Kelly)

Kathleen Seerey (Mrs. Redmond), St. Stephen's Green
Jenny Shanahan, City Hall; Prisoner
Mary Shannon
Hanna Sheehy-Skeffington
T. Simpson
Margaret Skinnider, St. Stephen's Green
Miss Smith
Josephine Spicer; Prisoner
Marion Stokes, Enniscorthy

Aoife Taafe
Nora Thornton
Kathleen Timoney
A. Tobin
Catherine Treston; Prisoner
S. Twomey

Bridie Walsh
Eileen Walsh, Father Mathew Hall

Margaret (Maggie) Walsh
Martha Walsh (Mrs. Murphy), Imperial Hotel
Mary Jo Walsh
Mary White, Enniscorthy
A. Wisely
Nancy Wyse Power

Unidentified Red Cross Nurse

1
Women Organising

Inghinidhe na hÉireann

On Easter Sunday 1900, a small group of women came together in Dublin to form Inghinidhe na hÉireann (Daughters of Erin). Despite their militant commitment to the struggle for Irish freedom from British rule, it is unlikely that many of them could have foreseen where that struggle would lead them exactly sixteen years later. Inghinidhe was the first attempt by nationalist women to organise themselves in almost two decades and was a response to the exclusion of women from all of the existing nationalist organisations. Their most famous member, Maud Gonne, was one of the outstanding political figures of the times, and instrumental in founding Inghinidhe. She was, however, not typical of the group's members, most of whom were women who worked for their living.

They were influenced by the suffrage and labour struggles in Britain and elsewhere, but drew deeply upon the experience of Irish history. Their aspirations as women had a distinctly Irish character and they looked for examples from within their own heritage, such as the Brehon laws, to give their struggle legitimacy. The members of Inghinidhe looked to an early Gaelic Ireland to provide a model of a society in which women could play their role in public life on an equal footing to men.

Perhaps their perceptions of life in ancient Ireland were idealised but, more importantly, they viewed freedom for Ireland and freedom for Irish women as inseparable. They were convinced that so long as Ireland was unfree Irish women would be unable to become free citizens; they were convinced also, that Britain would not cede Irish independence voluntarily.

The 'Three Great Movements'

Following the dissolution of the Ladies' Land League, women had not been allowed to join any of the Irish nationalist organisations, and there were no mixed-sex organisations until 1910. Women were, nevertheless, integrally involved in what Constance Markievicz called 'the three great movements' of the times — the struggle for land, the struggle for women's rights and the struggle of labour. These movements were inextricably intertwined and while influenced by developments internationally, were rooted in a deep-seated awareness of the dispossession of the Irish nation.

The Ladies' Land League was formed in 1881; between then and its forced dissolution in 1882 more than 5,000 women were members. However, even before the Ladies' Land League was organised, women were at the forefront of the land wars.

> Terrible scenes were common in 1880. In January of that year about five hundred women and girls barred the way to a process-server and his armed escort who had come to serve ejectment notices at Knockrichard, near Claremorris. Officers drew their swords and attacked the bareheaded and barefooted women who made a last stand of desperation. Some suffered sword thrusts and bayonet wounds, others were knocked down and trampled upon.[1]

Many of the women political activists, particularly in Dublin and Belfast, were involved in all three movements. Those fighting for women's social, political and economic rights focussed mainly on the campaign for suffrage, but did not limit themselves to demanding the vote. An important strand of the feminist movement identified closely with the struggles of the poor and dispossessed and in particular, championed the rights of working class women. Constance Markievicz, for instance, lent her support to a suffrage rally in London's Trafalgar Square in 1908, at which she defended the right of women to work in bars.

> There is a league for the abolition of barmaids, and it is an infamous league. They cannot abolish woman, take away her occupation and let her starve ... we are told that the bar is a bad place for women, but the Thames Embankment at night is far worse.[2]

The Irish Women Workers' Union had been formed in September 1911. But even prior to that women workers had learned the power of organisation. In August of that year, 3,000 women at the Jacob's biscuit factory in Dublin had gone on strike for higher wages and won. In the Great Lockout of 1913, when the workers of Dublin fought against the tyranny of their employers, women were involved; not just as wives and daughters, but as workers. As James Connolly later wrote:

> When that story is written ... it will tell of how the old women and the young girls, long crushed and enslaved, dared to risk all, even life itself, in the struggle to make life more tolerable, more free of the grinding tyranny of the soul-less Dublin employers ...[3]

The entire membership of the Irish Women Workers' Union came out on strike and remained out for six months. The women of Jacob's biscuit factory were among the most militant of the strikers in 1913. Many of the women who were later to join the Irish Citizen Army were young women who had been dismissed from Jacob's for their trade unionism.

Founding of Cumann na mBan

In the years immediately prior to World War I, the agitation for Home Rule was intensified, and it became increasingly clear that the Unionists were going to fight to maintain the union with Britain. The Ulster Volunteers, precursors of the Ulster Volunteer Force, were formed in 1912 after 400,000 men had signed a 'Solemn League and Covenant' against Home Rule;

women were not able to sign the Covenant, but 234,000 of them signed a 'Women's Declaration' at the same time. With the open military organisation and arming of the Unionists, the political climate made it possible for an Irish nationalist military organisation to be established. The Irish Volunteers were founded in November 1913, at the instigation of the Irish Republican Brotherhood (IRB).

The inaugural meeting of Cumann na mBan, formed as the women's organisation linked to the Volunteers, took place on 2 April, 1914. In May, Inghinidhe merged with Cumann na mBan, although they remained a separate branch. Not all members of the new organisation had a clearly defined philosophy of women's rightful place as equal members of a free Ireland, although many certainly did. By virtue of the fact, however, that they ventured into the public sphere — attending meetings, going on training exercises and travelling up and down the country, for example — they were breaking out of the confines of what was generally considered an acceptable role for women at the time. Some of the women of Cumann na mBan were conscious feminists and a minority insisted that equality required that they take on the same tasks as the men. Others were satisfied to apply the skills they had, or learn skills such as first aid, which were generally considered to be suitable for women. These differences of outlook, while subordinated to agreement on the practical tasks to be done, did not entirely disappear.

> Their first job was to initiate a Defence of Ireland fund for arming and equipping the Volunteers. They thought this a necessary step toward regaining for the women of Ireland the rights that belonged to them under the old Gaelic civilization, where sex was no bar to citizenship and where women were free to devote to the service of their country their every talent and capacity. There was some muttering about not being represented on the Volunteer Executive, but for the most part the women were devoted to the areas in which it was generally agreed they could be of the most practical use at the time, fundraising and first aid. Some of the women learned to handle guns, but the demonstrations

on setting up field kitchens and feeding the army were more popular.[4]

Louise Gavan Duffy, a founder of Cumann na mBan, did not think it necessary to assert women's independent interests through the new organisation. She described the alliance between feminists and non-feminists from her viewpoint.

> There were women on the committee who strongly supported the cause of women's rights and who had previously worked for the suffragettes. There were others who didn't share those opinions — but the affairs of the Volunteers were so important, so secretive and so necessary that we couldn't afford to divide our energies or our responsibilities. We put every other consideration aside and were ready to do whatever we were asked to do: messages, attending the wounded, supplying ammunition, any work which was needed. Perhaps there were women who took a more military role. It is the case I suppose that there were women who did just that but it wasn't part of the Cumann na mBan policy. Of course I am not describing the activities of the Citizen Army.[5]

Irish Citizen Army

The Irish Citizen Army (ICA) was formed as a labour defence force during the 1913 Dublin Lockout. Its members were mainly trade unionists and women members had equal rights and duties with the men, at least in principle. No formal distinction was made between male and female members and ICA women carried arms. Constance Markievicz, Helena Molony, Kathleen Lynn and Madeleine ffrench-Mullen were all ICA officers.

Constance Markievicz was a member of a well-known Ascendancy family, the Gore-Booths of Sligo. She first became active in the women's suffrage movement, and it was Helena Molony who suggested she join Inghinidhe na hÉireann. Markievicz was centrally involved in ICA activities during the 1913 Lockout and became well loved by the Dublin working class. A popular actress at the Abbey Theatre, Helena Molony took over as editor of the nationalist women's newspaper, *Bean na hÉireann,* in 1908. Kathleen Lynn was one of a small minority of Irish women who had not only managed to get a higher education but had excelled in a profession overwhelmingly dominated by men. She was prominent both as a surgeon and in the fight for women's political rights. It was through her experiences in the women's movement that she became convinced that if Irish women were to achieve equality it would be necessary to win national independence for Ireland. Madeleine ffrench-Mullen and Kathleen Lynn a few years later were the founders of the St. Ultan's children's hospital in Dublin.

A number of women who were members of the ICA were members of the Irish Transport and General Workers' Union. Some, such as Rosie Hackett, had worked in Jacob's biscuit factory, but had not been re-employed after the 1913 Lockout. Rosie worked in the printshop attached to Liberty Hall and was one of the workers who helped to print the Proclamation of the Irish Republic read out by Padraic Pearse at noon on Easter Monday 1916 from the steps of the GPO as the Rising began. Markievicz and Molony had helped to set up a shirt-making co-operative in Liberty Hall to give employment to women who could not find work after the Lockout. Jenny Shanahan, another ICA member, worked in the co-op, which was next to the print shop.

In the ICA, men and women did weapons training together, sometimes under women officers, and women participated in military lectures. The ICA had a miniature rifle range and both men and women used it to practise shooting. Both the Irish Volunteers and the ICA used the *Fianna Handbook*, written by Markievicz, considered to be the best training manual available. (Fianna Éireann was the republican youth organisation set up by Constance Markievicz, Bulmer Hobson and Helena Molony in 1908.)

Women took part in all the ICA's route marches, some of which lasted all night, making them scarcely a 'proper' activity for women at the time. The last route march before the Rising was sixteen miles long. As well as being important training exercises, route marches accustomed the police to the sight of armed mobilisations and thus lulled them into a degree of complacency about the possibllity of a genuine offensive.

It was not just in the ICA, however, that women took on a military role. Cumann na mBan in Belfast regularly held rifle practice and was confident enough to challenge the local Volunteers to a shooting contest. One member, Winifred Carney, who also belonged to the ICA, was known as a crack shot. Many other Cumann na mBan branches trained their members to use arms.

In a few cases women were admitted to membership of the Volunteers, possibly because of the influence of individual men, or the determination of individual women in specific situations. Kathleen Keyes McDonnell was a member of the Volunteers for some time before she founded a branch of Cumann na mBan in her area. When her husband, the leader of the Volunteers in Bandon, County Cork, was away, she sometimes deputised for him. Likewise, Margaret Skinnider joined the Glasgow Volunteers, although she operated as an ICA member when in Ireland. Even the highly secretive Irish Republican Brotherhood was not exclusively a male organisation. Robert Brennan, of Wexford, had insisted that his fiancée, Una Bolgar, be sworn in.

> When I was about to get married the pledge of secrecy I had given disturbed me. I felt I had no right to withhold from the lady who was to be my life partner, the fact that I was pledged to the cause. I could tell her, however, only if she was a member also. I put this up to the authorities and was so stubborn about it that Una was sworn into the organisation by the same Sean T. Kelly. I was told later that only one other woman had ever been admitted. I think it was Maud Gonne.[6]

It is likely that if there was in fact only one other female member of the IRB, it was Kathleen Clarke, rather than Maud Gonne. Clarke, who was married to the IRB leader Tom Clarke, wanted to accompany Tom to the GPO when he set off to fight in the Rising. She could not do so because she was under orders and the work she had been trusted with took precedence over everything else. Kathleen Clarke was entrusted with all the IRB membership lists and had responsibility to take care of the families of those killed or imprisoned for their part in the Rising. It is likely therefore, that she would have been sworn into the organisation.

Women from Diverse Backgrounds

Women were offering their services to the movement all over the country. Some, like Nora Connolly, came from republican or labour movement families. Connolly lived with her mother and the rest of her family in Belfast, earning her living as a seamstress. During the First World War she made items such as mattress covers for the British Army. Working on piecework allowed her to take time off for political work, although it meant working much harder to catch up. Nora was an organiser for Cumann na mBan in the Belfast area.

Many others, however, had no previous connections with the nationalist movement. Éilis Ní Chorra, for example, was not from a nationalist background: 'I knew nothing of the Irish movement and the traditions of nationality which had been kept alive by the "faithful few", the children and grandchildren of the Fenians.'[7] She was strongly affected by the wartime propaganda of the British, but not in the way that was intended.

> The war-mongering and flag-waving in Belfast disgusted me. I felt mad when I heard Irish girls talking about 'our' soldiers, saw them hobnobbing with khaki-clad men and selling flags to provide comforts for the troops. Then I felt fiercely Irish, and went around with a chip on my shoulder.[8]

In 1915, one of her brothers joined the Volunteers and suggested that she and her sister Kathleen attend O'Donovan Rossa's funeral. The funeral was the occasion of a massive demonstration of nationalist feeling; over 1,000 uniformed members of Cumann na mBan marched alongside all the other nationalist organisations. Later that year the two sisters joined Cumann na mBan and the Gaelic League. 'This meant a complete change in my life and the severing of many ties of friendship.'[9] Less than six months later, she would be standing in Liberty Hall, looking at a copy of the Proclamation of the Republic, still wet from the printing press.

The sisters had both had first aid training and physical drill at the technical college and so had no difficulties with the Cumann na mBan training. For the first time they heard Irish being spoken, and were drawn into Irish dancing. Éilis became a crack shot, although 'only with a miniature rifle — the service rifles were too precious to be used for practice.'[10]

It was not only in Ireland that women looked for an active part in the nationalist movement. Cumann na mBan branches were organised in several British cities where there were Irish populations. They sent food supplies during the Rising and a number of women travelled from Britain to participate — although most did not know until they got there that their journey was for more than training purposes. Margaret Skinnider was the most prominent of the British-based women involved in the Rising.

As a child Margaret Skinnider had emigrated from Ireland to Scotland with her family and had grown up in Glasgow. Skinnider was deeply involved in the campaign for women's suffrage there, but always thought of herself as Irish and joined both the Volunteers and Cumann na mBan. This 23 year old woman was determined to fight for her country when the chance came and became an excellent shot. She learned to shoot in one of the rifle clubs which the British organised so that women could help in the defence of the Empire. 'These clubs had sprung up like mushrooms and died just as quickly, but I kept on till I was a good marksman. I believed the opportunity would soon come to defend my own country.'[11]

While weapons training was important to many of the women, there were many equally important, though perhaps more mundane, jobs to be done.

First Aid

In the early years of the twentieth century career options for women who wanted to pursue a socially useful occupation and earn an independent livelihood were very restricted. Nursing, one of the few professions open to women, attracted large numbers of women of widely divergent political views. As the western world moved closer to war, the British government encouraged women to attend subsidised first aid classes and fostered the establishment of Red Cross societies. Irish women who had no intention of contributing to the British Empire's war effort seized the opportunity to develop their skills. Their reasoning was that first aid workers would be indispensable to an insurrection and first aid work was thus an eminently practical way of participating in the fight for Ireland's independence. Inghinidhe na hÉireann gave priority to both stretcher and arms drill. Some of the women took government-subsidised first aid classes, then gave the money they saved from the fees to the Volunteer movement.

In 1914, shortly after Cumann na mBan was established, efforts were made to get the organisation recognised as the Irish branch of the International Red Cross. The Red Cross stated, however, that it could not admit a group from a country without its own standing army and recommended that Cumann na mBan affiliate to the British Red Cross. This, of course, Cumann na mBan declined to do.

In some areas of Ireland there was rivalry between the Red Cross and Cumann na mBan. Kathleen Keyes McDonnell, a member of the Irish Volunteers, called a meeting in August 1914 to set up a Cumann na mBan branch in Bandon. The willingness of women to be active outside the domestic sphere is demonstrated by the fact that almost 300 women attended, although there seems to have been some confusion about the aims of the organisation. Many of those at the meeting were supporters of the union with Britain and only about 30 women joined up once Cumann na mBan's uncompromisingly nationalist stance was explained.

The next day Lady Bandon, who was organising the local Red Cross branch, wrote to McDonnell saying that the town was too small for two organisations. She offered McDonnell a place on the Red Cross committee if she would disband Cumann na mBan. McDonnell responded by inviting Lady Bandon to join Cumann na mBan instead. The unionist and Protestant Lady Bandon lost no time in appealing to the Catholic hierarchy for help. The next morning she visited the local canon and, without mentioning her correspondence with McDonnell, persuaded him to make an appeal from the pulpit for members to join the Red Cross. Then she went to the local convent and appealed to the mother superior for support. Soon McDonnell was summoned to receive a lecture from the Reverend Mother, who told her: 'Don't you see, my dear child, Almighty God put her in the position in which she is.' McDonnell was not intimidated.

> Astounded, I was tempted to tell her that Lady Bandon owed her position in the first instance to Elizabeth and secondly to Cromwell, but instead I replied coldly: 'And who do you think, Reverend Mother, put me in mine?'[12]

The following Sunday the formation of the Red Cross was announced at Mass.

> The Red Cross was launched with a great flutter of wings, supported by all those who had trooped out of our meeting in the Town Hall, and what was unknown in Bandon history up to that time, even prominent Catholics foregathered in the Allen Institute, notorious loyalist stronghold, and there attended classes and meetings in furtherance of Britain's war effort.[13]

Meanwhile, those women committed to the nationalist cause continued in their work. Local doctors and nurses gave classes in first aid. 'We were facilitated with full medical equipment for our purpose,' McDonnell recalled. 'One time we had the use of a whole skeleton. "Please pass the bones" became an amusing commonplace.'[14] A doctor from Dublin came to test the women and award certificates and Bandon Cumann na mBan was very proud to be the first professionally trained first aid unit in County Cork.

After World War I broke out, Cumann na mBan was encouraged by some supporters to apply again for recognition as the official Red Cross body in Ireland. With such recognition Cumann na mBan would have acquired a field hospital, but, at the same time, would have become tied to the British military. For this reason, no application was made to the International Red Cross headquarters in Geneva. Cumann na mBan did, however, claim the right to use the Red Cross emblem in first aid or hospital work. Later, during the 1916 Rising, the first aid units were careful to be clearly identified, but the Red Cross insignia afforded them no protection from the British forces.

First aid work and training were taken very seriously. The well-known actress Máire Nic Shiubhlaigh recounts in her autobiography how the Cumann na mBan branch she founded in Glasthule, Dublin spent much of its time in the early months of 1916 making first aid kits. She herself spent most of the week before that Easter at Volunteer headquarters in Dawson Street making kits.

A Dr Touhy lectured Cumann na mBan's Central Branch and Dr Kathleen Lynn gave lectures in first aid to men and women in the ICA. The classes were considered an important means to build comradeship between men and women volunteers. Endless evenings were spent in preparing medical kits and practising first aid up and down the country. Nora Connolly was in charge of an ambulance corps in Belfast; she gave lectures in first aid to men and women volunteers as well as to members of the republican scouting organisation Fianna Éireann. Belfast was the only area in which Fianna Éireann had a section for girls, possibly as a result of the influence of James Connolly and his daughters who had their home in the city.

In Limerick there was a strong Cumann na mBan organisation. Robert Monteith, a leader of the Limerick Volunteers, had great respect for the women's work.

> ... without their help the Volunteer movement would never have been the success it was. These women did not theorise, they did practical work. At Limerick they accompanied us on all field work in order to train the Red Cross section. Few field days went by without an accident, and whether they were called upon to treat cuts, abrasions, sprains or dislocations, they knew what should be done; they knew how to do it, and they did it.[15]

Fundraising

Fundraising was an important part of the work of the women volunteers. Each Cumann na mBan member was expected to raise the funds to equip one Volunteer member as well as herself. All sorts of events — céilís, concerts and the like — were held in every part of Ireland and considerable amounts of money were raised. Cumann na mBan contributed significantly to the funds that purchased large quantities of arms abroad. The first major importation of arms by nationalists became known as the Howth gunrunning. The guns were paid for partly by money raised by Cumann na mBan and partly through the efforts of the committee set up by Alice Stopford Green in London. Stopford Green advanced £1,500 of her own money.

2
Military and Political Preparations

Howth Gunrunning

During 1914 there was endless drilling of men and women, but only a very few functional weapons were available. It was Mary Spring-Rice, daughter of Lord Monteagle and niece of the British ambassador to the USA, who suggested that guns could be smuggled into Ireland on private yachts, whose wealthy owners would be unlikely to come under suspicion from the British. In the Spring of 1914, a small group, all Protestants, met in the London home of the historian Alice Stopford Green to work out the details of the plan. Mary Spring-Rice approached some of her friends about the use of their yachts. Some 1,500 rifles and 50,000 rounds of ammunition were to be shipped from Hamburg. Two yachts, the *Asgard* and the *Kelpie*, would rendezvous with a German ship off the Belgian coast and deliver the weapons to Ireland.

The *Asgard* was crewed by the novelist and former British civil servant, Erskine Childers, his wife Mary (Osgood), Mary Spring-Rice, Childers' friend Gordon Shephard, and two fishermen. The voyage began on 1 July 1914. Almost two weeks and many bouts of seasickness later, the crew successfully transferred its share of the arms to the *Asgard*.

> [T]he tug pulled up. "He's left you 900 [rifles] and 29,000 rounds," ... We looked at each other — how could we ever take them? We had only counted on 750, and they looked enormous. ... we stowed away feverishly to get them in. Once Molly put pieces of chocolate literally into our mouths, as we worked, and that kept us going until about 2 a.m. when the last box was heaved onto the deck and the last rifle stowed down the companion.[1]

Mary woke on 13 July wondering if the previous night's work had been a dream. 'However down below was the solid reality

— saloon, cabin and passage were all built up two and a half feet high with guns, and there was no illusion about the bruises one got as one crawled about on them.'[2]

On Thursday the 16th, Mary recorded events thus:

> Sixteen days at sea now and the bread locker is beginning to run very low and we are fearfully economical of water. Molly protests if I wash more than once a day, but with grease from cooking, black from washing potatoes, and oil from the fo'castle it becomes necessary sometimes. The cargo below has curtailed the air space considerably, and one spends as much time as possible on deck ... After dinner a fresh breeze sprang up and we beat along past Devonport, and to my horror got caught up in among the fleet. They seemed to be executing some night manouevres and were all round us with their great lights towering up; it would have been very picturesque if one had been looking on from a safe position on shore. There was one awful moment when a destroyer came very near. I stood holding up the stern light on the starboard side watching her get nearer and nearer, with my heart in my mouth, then mercifully at the last moment she changed her course and passed us by. Then the big jib had to be shifted and the jib sheet got lost under the dinghy, and Molly and I had to fish for it lying flat on the deck and wriggling under the dinghy. By the time we were clear of the fleet and excursions over it was 1 a.m. and I was glad to get to bed.[3]

At last, on 26 July, the *Asgard* sailed into Howth harbour and unloaded its cargo safely.

> The Volunteers were armed at last. I got ashore with my luggage and was warmly greeted by The O'Rahilly, Eoin MacNeill and others: one was in uniform and looking quite martial. Then the Volunteers formed up on the quay with their rifles; the Fianna took charge of the ammunition, and they all gave ringing cheers for the yacht and her owners, and several eager Volunteers jumped on board to help to hoist the mainsail.[4]

Some hours later at Constance Markievicz's house, Fianna members arrived with some of the guns. It was not the safest place to keep them, and Nora Connolly, who was staying at the house with her sister Ina, went to the Volunteer office for instructions. Liam Mellowes sent her back to the cottage with two Volunteers, who were to move the guns in a taxi. Nora suggested to the Volunteers that the taxi would come under less suspicion if the women took over the role of escorting the weapons. 'The girls piled in, the discomfort forgotten in the thought that the rifles were safe.'[5] It occurred to Nora to return to the Volunteer office, and 'ask Liam does he want us to sit on any more rifles'.[6] The young women spent the rest of the day sitting on guns and were rewarded with one each for their efforts.

Another woman involved in the gunrunning was Molly O'Reilly. Aged 15, she was already a member of the ICA. She had attended Irish dancing classes at Liberty Hall since the age of eight and had helped in the kitchens during the 1913 Lockout. Her experiences during this period had a very strong influence on her political outlook. When the guns were landed at Howth, Molly took charge of a handcart-load, which she pushed up Gardiner Street to her home. Unknown to her family, she hid the weapons for a time under her father's bed. Molly's family was opposed to her political activities and rather than give up her involvement, she soon afterwards left her family home. Molly would have the honour of lifting the Republican flag over Liberty Hall on Palm Sunday, 1916.

Armaments

The manufacture of bombs for use in a rising began in 1915. 'Dozens of enthusiastic women and girls worked, during their spare time, at various tasks connected with the manufacture of cartridges, bullets and bombs. The whole basement of Liberty Hall became one big munitions works.'[7]

The women's co-operative at Liberty Hall started producing haversacks and bandoliers, and an attempt was made to make a machine gun.

> Working long and hard right up to the eve of the Rising, they managed to get the gun ready for service. The problem of getting a cartridge belt perfectly adjusted to the gun had then to be tackled. Women worked all night — up to 6 a.m. on Easter Sunday morning — trying to devise a belt that would work smoothly without catching.[8]

Helena Molony explained that the machine gun belt, 'gave us women headaches because of the extreme accuracy of the measurements required. It was homemade as were all the bombs and hand grenades which the Citizen Army was accumulating.'[9]

> Firearms of every description were being acquired, an armoury room was set aside for sorting out equipment, preparing ammunition, manufacturing hand grenades, and so on. It was evident to all members of the Citizens Army that the situation was growing more serious from day to day.[10]

Armaments were stockpiled all over the city. Even though it was under constant surveillance, Constance Markievicz's house contained all sorts of weapons, hidden in every possible place. Nora Foley, a member of a Dublin republican family, described how her Fairview home too, was 'a regular arsenal of bombs which had been made on the premises, dynamite, gelignite, rifles, bayonets, ammunition and what not.'[11]

Éilis Uí Chonail tells how for some time small arms were imported from Sheffield labelled as 'cutlery'. A shipment was discovered in Dublin port and Dublin Castle was informed, but in the meantime Volunteer headquarters was also notified. Three members of Cumann na mBan rushed to the scene and saved the entire shipment of 110 revolvers and ammunition.

Another source of weapons was through raids on British army depots. One meticulously planned raid was on the British Auxiliary Defence Force, at Sutton Golf Club, County Dublin. Kathleen Lynn drove her car to Sutton to pick up the arms. Unfortunately on this occasion the 'guns' turned out to be useless wooden imitations; two of them subsequently hung at Markievicz's Dublin home, Surrey House, as mementoes.

Constance Markievicz heard of Margaret Skinnider's work in Glasgow Cumann na mBan and invited her to spend Christmas 1915 in Dublin. Skinnider went in the hope of finding out if there was any hope of a rising in the coming spring. She did not go empty-handed — or rather empty-hatted!

> Leaning back in a steamer chair, with my hat for a pillow, I dropped asleep. That I ever awakened was a miracle. In my

hat I was carrying to Ireland detonators for bombs and the wires were wrapped around me under my coat. That was why I had not wanted to go to a stateroom where I might run into a hot water pipe or an electric wire which might set them off. But pressure, they told me when I reached Dublin, is just as dangerous, and my head had been resting heavily on them all night![12]

Margaret Skinnider took part in a number of raids during her visits to Ireland.

The need for explosives was great and I took part in a number of expeditions to obtain them. One night we raided a ship lying in the river ... I was standing guard ... a policeman came slowly towards me. He had his dark-lantern and, catching sight of me, flashed it in my face. He stared, but said nothing. No doubt he was wondering what a decently dressed girl was doing in that part of town at such an hour.[13]

Intelligence Gathering

Margaret Skinnider was a mathematics teacher. During her 1915 visit to Dublin she told Constance Markievicz about her love of the subject and about the course in calculus she had just completed. Markievicz was responsible for drawing up all the maps for the Rising and for preparing plans of all the strategic points to be taken over. Markievicz asked Skinnider if she could draw a plan of Beggars Bush Barracks from observation in case a decision was ever made to dynamite it, but omitted to mention to Skinnider that two male volunteers had already failed in the task. When completed, Skinnider's plan was shown to Connolly, who declared it to be very good. 'But the test I had been put to was, it seemed, not merely a test of my ability to draw maps and figure distances. From that day I was taken into the confidence of the leaders of the movement.'[14]

Skinnider worked as a member of the Citizen Army when she was in Dublin. During this Christmas visit, James Connolly visited Markievicz's home one evening in a particularly expansive mood. Markievicz explained to Skinnider, now very much part of the trusted leadership circle, that word had come from America about plans for a further shipment of guns from Germany. This meant that the Rising would definitely go ahead at Easter. That Christmas, Thomas MacDonagh gave Margaret Skinnider a revolver, treasured by her until it was confiscated by the British. Before long Skinnider had to return to Glasgow, but she took leave from her teaching job in order to be in Dublin again in time for the Rising, which she now knew was planned for Easter.

For months prior to the insurrection, women were detailed to watch military barracks across the country. On Easter Saturday, four women were detailed to watch the magazine fort at Phoenix Park. They were to observe the number in the guard, when the guard changed and any visits by officers. Nora Foley was one of those involved.

> Two of us went up and lounged about the place for some hours chatting with the soldiers on guard, thereby gleaning all the information required ... we felt very satisfied with what we had learned and strolled off shortly after the other two girls appeared on the scene, without exchanging any sign of recognition with them.[15]

The usefulness of the women's prior intelligence work was proved in many — and sometimes unforeseen — ways once the Rising began. On Easter Tuesday, during the retreat from St. Stephen's Green, ICA member Lily Kempson handed over a prisoner to Captain Frank Robbins. The man had been arrested because one of the women recognised him as a British soldier from the barracks she had been watching.

Couriers

In the course of the preparations for the Rising, the women officers of the Citizen Army discussed what they should wear. Constance Markievicz opted for riding breeches, which she combined with one of Michael Mallin's old uniform jackets. On marches before the Rising, however, she decided to wear a skirt over the breeches, as there seemed little point in provoking scandal over the question of dress. Margaret Skinnider, who could pass for a boy and who, as a courier, would spend much of her time on a bicycle, planned to wear breeches also. In fact, Skinnider wore a dress when engaged in courier work during the Rising, because a 'girl on a bicycle' was less likely to be challenged than a boy. She did however don a uniform at other times. The other women chose to wear the less practical, but socially more acceptable and certainly less conspicuous long skirts of the day. These did create some problems once the insurrection began. One of the women tore her skirt while climbing over the gates during the occupation of the Dublin City Hall and other women found them awkward when it became necessary to climb over barricades or through windows and holes in walls.

Often it was precisely the fact that they were less likely to attract attention than men — so long as they dressed conventionally — that gave the women an advantage for the work they had to do. The task of moving guns and ammunition around the country was one of the more dangerous jobs carried out by women. Voluminous skirts in this case came in quite handy. The women acted as couriers all over the country as well as abroad, and made many perilous journeys carrying weapons and vital messages.

In December 1914, Nora Connolly travelled to the United States on a mission that, had she been discovered, would have resulted in five people — including herself, her father, and Constance Markievicz — being hanged for treason. Frank Robbins tells how after the Rising Nora disclosed to him the purpose of her trip.

> Around 1915 it was well known that concrete ships were being built in the shipyards in Belfast and presumably in other shipbuilding ports. Information leaked out that these ships were to be used for the blocking of the Zeebrugge Canal which was the operational headquarters of the German submarine command. Such a scheme, if successful, would have blocked the U-boat exits and Connolly thought the news important enough to warrant sending his daughter to New York to see John Devoy and have him arrange an

interview for her with Count Bernstorff, the German ambassador.[16]

Nora was also involved in a later mission to England. On 26 March 1916, a Friday evening, Liam Mellowes, a leading member of the Volunteers, was arrested at the Athenry home of Julia Morrissey, the founder of Cumann na mBan in the town. Mellowes, who was under a banning order and transported to England, managed to send word of his destination to Seán MacDiarmada, a member of the Military Council. James Connolly sent his daughter Nora and Mellowes' brother Barney to England to smuggle Liam back to Ireland. The following Sunday, Barney and Liam met in a pub and exchanged clothes. Liam slipped out and met Nora, who was waiting in a taxi. By the next day Connolly and Liam Mellowes were in Glasgow where, with the help of a woman called Maggie Eakins, Connolly obtained clothing from a priest. By Wednesday, accompanied by Winifred Carney, Liam was on his way to Dublin. Soon he was back in Galway, where he was needed to lead the Rising in the west.

For some time, complex negotiations had been in progress to obtain further shipments of arms from Germany. These negotiations involved sending messages from Ireland to Germany via Irish supporters in the USA. The old Fenian John Devoy in New York and Roger Casement in Germany were key figures in these operations. The plan was that arms would arrive by boat (the *Aud*) off the shores of Kerry on the Thursday before Easter. They would be landed by Volunteers from Munster and distributed around the country. Munster woman Kathleen Timoney, although heavily pregnant at the time (she gave birth on 3 May), was in contact with the Military Council in Dublin and made preliminary arrangements for signalling the *Aud* on its arrival.

When the Military Council of the IRB realised that the arms expected from Germany could not be landed secretly, it was urgent that supporters in America be informed of their changed plans. Philomena (Mimi) Plunkett, the sister of Joseph Plunkett, was sent to New York with a message, arriving on 14 April.

The message she carried was: 'Arms must not be landed before the night of Easter Sunday, 23rd. This vital. Smuggling impossible.' She also brought information about arrangements for wireless signals to be sent to the vessel when it got close to Ireland. This information was then telegraphed from the US to Berlin, but by that time the *Aud* had already sailed for Ireland; it carried no telegraph receiver.

> Mrs Plunkett was in New York at the time of her daughter's arrival, seeking aid of the Catholic Church in America for the canonization of Oliver Plunkett, who belonged to the same branch of the family, so that the coming of Philomena seemed a natural thing, and the British government had no suspicion of her real object.[17]

(The Countess Plunkett was an accomplished linguist, artist and art historian. After the crushing of the Rising and the arrest of her husband and three sons, she went from official to official for news of them until she was herself taken prisoner. She was held for five weeks, transferred from one prison to another and denied news of her family. She was then placed under a banning order along with her husband and not allowed to return to Ireland for several years. Her oldest son, Joseph, was executed; two younger sons, George and John, were sentenced to death but their sentences wer commuted to 10 years imprisonment.)

Cultural Revival

Cultural activities held a central place in the life of the nationalist movement. The 'Gaelic revival' brought together intellectuals and working class people and many of the leading figures in the country's literary and dramatic renaissance were deeply involved also in political and military activities. The Ard Craobh ('central branch') of Cumann na mBan organised fundraising concerts every second Sunday. Women also played a prominent role in ICA cultural events and entertainments, which were explicitly nationalist in character, at Liberty Hall.

Sunday night concerts were a regular event in Liberty Hall, the headquarters of both the ICA and the Irish Transport and General Workers' Union, as were dramatic presentations. Josie

Pollard and Katie Barrett were members of the Liberty Players. Emily Norgrove, Molly O'Reilly and Mary Hyland were popular singers. Maeve Cavanagh also took an active part in the dramatic presentations. She was a leading member of the ICA and several of her poems were published in *Workers' Republic*, including one entitled 'Call to Arms'. James Connolly called her the 'poetess of the revolution'. (Cavanagh continued to write nationalist poetry after the Rising.) One of the Liberty Players' productions was James Connolly's own play, 'Under Which Flag?', with Katie Barrett taking a leading role.

Agitation

Markievicz received a request that she attend the Fianna Festival in Tralee on 26 March to lecture on the Fenian Rising. But the authorities very quickly served on her an order under the Defence of the Realm Act, forbidding her to speak at the meeting in Kerry.

Markievicz was eager to go regardless, but Connolly ordered her not to leave Dublin, as she was too valuable to the work in hand to risk arrest. Markievicz had been appointed by the Military Council as James Connolly's 'ghost'. This meant that as his deputy she had to be sufficiently aware of the plans to take over his work if he was captured or otherwise put out of action. It was agreed that Marie Perolz, who was of a similar build to Markievicz, would deliver the speech instead. Perolz, a member of Cumann na mBan as well as of the ICA, worked very closely with Markievicz and Connolly and was the registered owner of the nationalist paper *The Spark*.

Two detectives travelled with Perolz on the train, believing her to be Constance Markievicz. A guard of honour met her at the station. When Perolz arived in Kerry, she informed the local Cumann na mBan leader and Austin Stack, leader of the Volunteers, of her true identity. The detectives came to her hotel and interrogated her. 'The Volunteers paraded ready to start a fight if a hair of the Countess' head was touched.'[18] At the meeting Marie Perolz read out the exclusion order, then read Markievicz's speech. 'The effect was electrical. The authorities could certainly congratulate themselves on helping to make the meeting a huge success and, as the main purpose of the gathering was to raise funds to buy munitions for the coming Rising, this was greatly appreciated.'[19]

Marie Perolz was still in Tralee when the *Aud* arrived off Tralee Bay with Roger Casement on board, but she did not hear of it until she was on her way back to Dublin.

During these final months and weeks of preparation, Liberty Hall was the scene of constant activity. The day-to-day work of the trade union movement went on side by side with preparations for the Rising.

A week before Good Friday, 1916, the printshop in Liberty Hall was raided by the police. Rosie Hackett went into Liberty Hall to warn James Connolly. When he arrived on the scene, Helena Molony was standing with her automatic pistol trained on the police. They were there to seize documents, but had no search warrant and eventually went away to get one. Nora Connolly and Constance Markievicz decided that a large presence of ICA members was needed to defend Liberty Hall as it was not only the headquarters of the revolution but also housed the munitions factory and the printing press. They hurriedly filled out 250 mobilisation orders. Within an hour of the mobilisation order, over 150 ICA members flooded into the union headquarters. Margaret Skinnider gives a vivid account of the effectiveness of the mobilisation: 'On the run, slipping into uniform coats as they ran; several from the tops of buildings where they were at work, others from underground. More than one, thinking this was an occasion of some seriousness, instantly threw up their jobs.'[20]

The police returned with a warrant and searched the printshop but found no documents. At the door into Liberty Hall itself, James Connolly was standing with a gun in his hand; the police made no attempt to enter. Both the men and women guarding Liberty Hall carried weapons. Molony commented: 'We were all armed, which fact helped to make up the Inspector's mind as to the undesirability of raiding Liberty Hall for which he had no warrant.'[21] After this, an armed guard was kept on Liberty Hall, and especially the printing press, twenty-four hours a day.

Secrecy

By the week before Easter, most members of the Citizen Army were aware that the Rising was to take place during Easter weekend. By contrast, most of the Irish Volunteers and Cumann na mBan members knew a rising was imminent, but were not told that a date had been set. Even Tomás MacCurtain and Terence McSwiney who were the leaders of the movement in Munster were not fully informed of the plans. When the Rising did start, many Volunteers around the country did not know until news leaked out later in the week. Even in Dublin, activists were caught off-guard. This confusion was to have disastrous consequences.

Cumann na mBan member Leslie Price remembered:

> We had no knowledge of the imminence of the situation. Well, I suppose Mrs Clarke [Kathleen Clarke, wife of Tom Clarke, a member of the Military Council] and those senior officers would have had, but the ordinary rank and file didn't. There was one thing, however, that struck me and gave me the idea that there was something serious coming off. On the eve of Palm Sunday there was a very large céilí organised... I remember quite well seeing Seán MacDiarmada and all those down there, and I said to myself, 'tis like a final reunion they were having.'[22]

Indeed, the céilí had in fact been organised to cover a meeting of the Military Council. Kathleen Clarke and Sorcha MacMahon, another prominent Cumann na mBan member, were the only other people who were aware of the real reason it was being held and Clarke tells of an objection from Con Colbert against a céilí being held in Lent.

> He was deeply religious, and did not think it right. I could not explain the reason for it to him, so I told him not to be so squeamish and to dance while he could, as he might be dancing at the end of a rope one of these days. I fear I shocked him, and I was sorry the minute the words were out of my mouth. I was sorry for having been so flippant, but I was under a great strain at the time.[23]

(Con Colbert was to lead the Marrowbone Lane Garrison during the Rising and was executed on 8 May 1916.)

The previous Thursday, Leslie Price had been told by a prominent member of Cumann na mBan that the Rising was to start on Easter Sunday. 'I realised that it was a frightful error on her part, to tell me, a very junior member of Cumann na mBan, and I didn't say a word to my two brothers [who were both Volunteers].'[24]

It was Marie Perolz, a member of both the ICA and Cumann na mBan, who told Julia Grenan that the Rising was definitely on. Julia worked as a furrier in one of the big Dublin stores. She and her friend Elizabeth O'Farrell had been inseparable friends since primary school. O'Farrell had joined Inghinidhe in 1906 at the age of 16; Grenan joined also. On the eve of the Rising they were called to Liberty Hall. Constance Markievicz introduced them to Connolly and told him they could be trusted with any work. Connolly decided to attach them to the Citizen Army. The two women apparently believed that their efforts would be more valued by the ICA than by the Volunteers: 'We saw no objection to that because the Volunteers weren't taking any notice of us, didn't care whether we were there or not.'[25]

Raising the Flag

On Palm Sunday, 16 April 1916, a ceremony took place at Liberty Hall. It was exactly one week before the day the Military Council (controlled by the IRB) had set for the Rising to commence. James Connolly intended, according to historian R. M. Fox, to make a challenge to 'all the ideas and loyalties which clung round the British connection'.[26] Thousands of people crowded into Beresford Square to observe the events.

The Citizen Army assembled in formation in front of Liberty Hall; the Boy Scouts and the Fintan Lalor Pipe Band took their places beside them. James Connolly appeared in military uniform for the first time, with Commandant Michael Mallin and Lieutenant Markievicz on either side of him. The colour party consisted of sixteen young men, while 15-year-old Molly

O'Reilly, a member of the Irish Women Workers' Union, carried the green flag to the centre of the square. With much music and ceremony the flag was borne into Liberty Hall, and a few minutes later Molly O'Reilly had it flying above the building. (This flag, the one flown over the GPO and other flags used during the Rising were made by Mrs Mary Shannon, a machinist in the Liberty Hall shirt-making cooperative.)

> There was a breathless hush and then thousands of people packed about the quays and on the bridge, saw the Green Flag of Ireland with the golden harp upon it, fluttering in the wind. This may not seem like much today but at that time it was an inspiration to all who stood for Irish independence. By some it was regarded as the first blow in the Rising.[27]

Final Preparations

During the final days of anxious preparation, women travelled up and down the country, delivering messages to and from the leadership in Dublin and the leaders in the regions. Communications were difficult because known activists were under constant police surveillance. It was necessary that the couriers be known to and trusted by those sending and receiving messages if difficulties and delays were to be avoided.

Agnes Ryan, a teacher at the Dominican High School in Belfast, was sent to see Seán MacDiarmada of the Military Council to arrange a meeting for Denis McCullough, who was then President of the IRB and who was responsible for the Belfast mobilisation.

On Monday, the 17th, Brigid Foley travelled to Cork (a four and a half hour train journey) with a message from Seán MacDiarmada to Tomás MacCurtain. She returned immediately with the reply. On Wednesday 19th she went back to Cork and again returned with an answer.

At Eamonn and Áine Ceannt's Dublin home, women couriers arrived at intervals throughout Thursday 20 April. (Captain Eamonn Ceannt led the contingent to Marrowbone Lane. A member of the Military Council, he was executed 8 May 1916.) Each had a private meeting with the Ceannts and left carrying dispatches with orders for the Rising. One of these was delivered by Mrs Fahy to Athenry. It read: 'Collect the premiums 7 p.m. Sunday. P. H. Pearse.'

Meanwhile, the work of making munitions, first aid kits, food and other supplies was stepped up. Insurrection necessitated countless tiny tasks, too. During the week Lily O'Brennan went to a shop on Eden Quay and purchased tricolour bunting, then brought it to a friend who had a sewing machine and who had agreed to make a flag for the Fourth Battalion of the Volunteers.

A large team spent Good Friday making bombs. They discovered that a large quantity of 'sparrow hail' had not been melted down. It was brought to Liberty Hall where moulds were made and the lead was turned into slugs to fit shotguns. It was tedious work, but men, women and children worked in shifts. The job, which had been thought impossible, was done in four days.

On Saturday, Lily O'Brennan, who was a sister of Áine Ceannt, delivered a dispatch from Eamonn Ceannt which outlined the arrangements for the care of the dependents of Volunteers killed or imprisoned. Kathleen Clarke was entrusted with all the important plans and decisions of the IRB along with lists of members, and funds to provide for families who lost their breadwinners. After the Rising it was to her that released prisoners reported. Kathleen's husband, the Fenian Tom Clarke, one of the leaders of the IRB, was a signatory of the Proclamation. He was executed following the Rising, as was Kathleen's brother, Edward Daly. Despite this tremendous personal loss, her own work never faltered.

Arrivals from Britain

Women resident in London, Liverpool and Glasgow participated in the Rising. On Thursday night, a group of Cumann na mBan women arrived in Dublin from Liverpool. Rose Ann Murphy, Peggy and Frances Downey, Anastasia MacLoughlin, Kathleen Murphy and Kathy Dornan had made the journey believing they were to attend a training camp. They met their leader, Nora Thornton, who was waiting for them in Dublin, and other comrades who had come home from Britain to join the Rising. Grace O'Sullivan was part of the London contingent.

The Glasgow contingent included Margaret Skinnider who arrived on Thursday. She went directly to Liberty Hall and was immediately set to work making cartridges. 'We melted down small shot, moulded large shot and closed the cartridges again.'[28] That evening she was given a despatch to take to Belfast.

She did not know where to find the man who was to receive the message, so it was necessary to go first to Nora Connolly's house on the Falls Road. She arrived in the city by train at about 2 a.m., and was obliged to ask a RIC man what tram to take. When she reached Connolly's house, it was a long time before anyone answered her knocks. No one had been in bed, however. The entire household had spent the previous few days working almost round the clock, preparing first aid kits and other equipment. At about 5 a.m. as workers were beginning to come out of nearby houses to go to their jobs, Nora Connolly and Margaret Skinnider left the house to deliver the despatch.

When Skinnider returned to Dublin later that Good Friday, the Connolly family went with her. In order not to arouse suspicion, they took only a few cases, as if they were going on holiday.

> This was not an easy leave-taking, for there was a fair chance of the house being sacked and burned. Mrs Connolly went about, picking up little things that would go in her trunk but the absence of which would not be noticed if any inquisitive policeman came in to see whether anything suspicious was going on. As we left, none of them looked back or gave any show of feeling.[29]

On the same day, the Ard Craobh of Cumann na mBan met at its office on Parnell Square to give its members orders for the Sunday mobilisation. The Central Branch was the original branch of the organisation. Kathleen Clarke was President and Sorcha MacMahon, Secretary. Among its first members were Miss A O'Rahilly, Máire Ní Riáin (Min Ryan), Elizabeth Bloxam, Áine Ceannt, Louise Gavan Duffy, Niamh Plunkett, Jenny Wyse Power and Mary S. Walsh.

Developments in Munster

Feverish preparations were also taking place outside Dublin. Mary MacSwiney, who was president of Cumann na mBan in Cork, spent the week before Easter preparing food and accommodation, as well as arranging for the care and maintenance of the dependents of Volunteers and overseeing arrangements for the work her members would have to do.

In March, Austin Stack had warned Bandon Cumann na mBan founder Kathleen McDonnell to expect something to happen at Easter. The 'expectation of arms was an open secret,'[30] she later wrote. A fortnight before Easter Seán MacCurtain sent the McDonnells a message 'to be ready for Easter'.[31] In all of Cork city and county, the McDonnells' car was the only one always available to the Volunteers. They now had it standing by, ready to collect the arms expected from Germany. Alice Cashel was given the difficult task of organising sufficient cars for the Sunday mobilisation of the Munster Volunteers.

On Thursday, the *Aud*, carrying the German guns on which the success of the Rising might depend, approached the Kerry coast. The German captain had been instructed to deliver the cargo between 20 and 23 April. He was unaware that the republican leadership had attempted to delay the landing until the 23rd, Easter Sunday. During the feverish preparations now being made for the Rising, it apparently occurred to no-one in Ireland that the shipment might arrive before then.

Meanwhile, in the early hours of Good Friday Roger Casement and two other men had arrived via a German submarine and landed at Banna Strand. Casement's two companions went on to Tralee, but Casement himself was swiftly arrested. The *Aud* had been spotted and followed by British naval vessels. On Saturday morning the *Aud*'s skipper scuttled the ship and its precious cargo at the entrance to Cobh harbour.

At 10 p.m. on Good Friday, Seán Nolan brought the order to Bandon for the Volunteers to mobilise with three days' rations. The McDonnells' car was to go to Cork to be at the disposal of MacCurtain and MacSwiney. William McDonnell was ill when the order arrived, and authority for the car was delegated to his wife Kathleen. It was arranged that she would phone Seán MacCurtain for final instructions on Saturday morning.

On Easter Saturday William McDonnell was too ill to drive and Kathleen phoned Seán MacCurtain stating that another driver was needed. She did not realise that the call had been intercepted and she was in fact talking to a detective. When the newspaper arrived with a report of the seizure of the arms shipment and the arrest of 'a stranger of unknown nationality',[32] she rang MacCurtain again. He was angry that she had not rung earlier; it then became clear that the previous call had been intercepted. Eventually, however, they were able to get the car safely into the hands of the Volunteer leaders in Cork.

3

Mobilisation and Countermand

Whilst the activists continued to work flat out on preparations for the imminent Rising, divisions within the leadership of the Volunteers began to come to a head with what were to be disastrous consequences.

On the Thursday before Easter (20 April), members of the IRB circulated a document purporting to be a British government order for the disarming of the Volunteers. This document is now widely considered to have been a forgery. The intention apparently, was to provoke the Volunteers into action.

Eoin MacNeill, although not a member of the IRB, had been elected as leader of the Volunteers with the organisation's agreement because they wished the Volunteers to be attractive to the broadest possible membership. MacNeill was not, however, told of the IRB's plans for a rising. He believed that the Volunteers were not yet ready to take on the much stronger British military forces. The IRB-dominated Military Council calculated that MacNeill would not allow the Volunteers to be disarmed without a fight. Thus it was hoped to draw in those Volunteers who might not have been prepared to initiate offensive military action. What they did not anticipate was what MacNeill and other members of the Volunteer leadership who shared his outlook would do when they discovered the deception.

On Easter Thursday, MacNeill and the Military Council would both issue orders for an Easter Sunday mobilisation. When MacNeill learned later that day that an insurrection was planned, he issued orders to cancel the mobilisation. When informed about the plans to land arms openly on Easter Sunday, MacNeill once again believed that it would be necessary to fight. He issued orders reversing his first countermand on Friday afternoon, before the countermand order had even been received by Volunteer units in many areas of the country. When news came of the loss of the arms and Casement's arrest, MacNeill moved once again to stop the mobilisations. The Military Council agreed with the cancellation of action on Easter Sunday, but independently issued orders for the fight to commence on Monday. This series of conflicting orders was sent around the country by couriers in cars, on bicycles and trains; in some cases messages were delivered after others which had been subsequently issued. Inevitably, the result was confusion and disruption, ensuring that any possibility of an effective mobilisation outside Dublin was lost. Throughout the country — and even in the capital city itself — the divisions in the leadership meant a considerable section of the Volunteer movement were left out of the fight.

Mobilisation: Orders and Countermands

Eoin MacNeill, the official leader of the Volunteers, believing that the British were going to move against the Volunteers, issued an order that the Volunteers were to prepare to take defensive action. This order was made with the agreement of the IRB leaders. On Thursday evening, Bulmer Hobson and Ginger O'Connell (members of the Volunteer Executive who shared MacNeill's views) discovered orders were going out for an insurrection on Easter Sunday and went immediately to MacNeill's house. MacNeill, convinced that a rising had no chance of success, went straight to Pearse's home and confronted him; Pearse then acknowledged that the IRB planned to start a rising.

In the early hours of Friday morning, MacNeill prepared to issue an order countermanding Pearse's orders which had been sent round the country the day before. That afternoon MacNeill sent Ginger O'Connell to Cork to take charge of the Munster Volunteers, Munster being one of the best organised areas outside Dublin, though the Volunteers there were almost without arms or ammunition. After his meeting with the Munster leadership, however, O'Connell did not attempt to take control; he had by this time been ordered to go instead to Wexford and take command there, perhaps because that was where IRB members Robert and Una Brennan were in the leadership. Alice Cashel was astonished when she was informed that the transport system she had organised for the Sunday mobilisation would no longer be necessary. By the time Ginger O'Connell had delivered these orders to Cork, they had already been revoked in Dublin.

On Friday morning, before the countermand had been distributed, Thomas MacDonagh and Seán MacDiarmada went to MacNeill and managed to persuade him that it was now too late to stop the Rising; they told him of the arms coming from Germany (none of the Dublin leaders yet knew that the *Aud* had been intercepted that morning.) In these circumstances he agreed, there would be no choice; a fight would then be inevitable. On Friday afternoon, MacNeill issued an order that the mobilisation planned for Sunday would proceed. This order would not reach Cork until the early hours of Saturday morning.

On Saturday, word that the *Aud* was sunk and Casement arrested reached Dublin. MacNeill was alarmed and now convinced that the Castle document was a forgery. The insurrection was not to begin until 7pm the following day, so he believed there was still time to call it off. Late that night, MacNeill issued an order cancelling all orders for 'special action' the next day. Min Ryan was one of several messengers who carried this order to units around the country. A second, more detailed order prohibiting all Volunteer movements that day, was printed in the *Sunday Independent*.

The Situation in the North

On Saturday afternoon the Belfast contingent consisting of 132 male Volunteers and six women of Cumann na mBan — Nora and Ina Connolly, Éilis Ní Chorra, her sister Kathleen, another woman called Éilis and Nell Gordon — travelled to Tyrone. (Many years later, Nora Connolly recollected that there were eight women from Belfast in all, whom she names as her sister Ina and herself, the Corr sisters, Bridie Farrell, Lizzie Allen, Kathleen Murphy and 'a girl called O'Neill'.) The Belfast Volunteers were under orders to link up with other northerners in Coalisland and then go to Galway to fight. There was to be no fighting in Ulster, James Connolly having assured the northern Volunteers that Ulster would be 'seen to' later. Several hundred Volunteers were gathered in a barn in Coalisland. Nora Connolly described the scene:

> The local organiser in Coalisland had gathered all his group in a big barn — and I stood still as it reminded me of all the things I'd read in books of the rendezvous of rebels. There they were, all around the walls, men sitting and waiting with their rifles and their bandoliers. It was extraordinary to see them there in the faint glimmer of a small oil lamp waiting for the word.[1]

In Coalisland, they received MacNeill's countermand of the mobilisation. The Tyrone leadership, which recognised MacNeill as the ultimate authority, refused to move their forces outside Tyrone.

Belfast leaders, Denis McCullough, President of the IRB, Dr MacCartan and a Miss Owens travelled to Dublin on Saturday night and were told by Tom Clarke that the Rising would go ahead on Sunday; there was no change of orders. The Belfast leaders, however, felt that they could not proceed without Tyrone. On Easter Sunday, the 132 Belfast men got on a train in Cookstown and went home. Most of them were soon arrested.

Nora Connolly was sure that whatever happened elsewhere, there would be a fight in Dublin. She refused to return to Belfast and the other Cumann na mBan members agreed with her decision to go to Dublin. Thus, the Belfast members of Cumann na mBan under 23 year old Nora Connolly's command became the only organised group from Ulster to take part in the Rising.

They reached the city about 5 a.m. on Easter Sunday and went directly to Liberty Hall. Nora Connolly insisted that her father be woken immediately and gave him the first news of what was now happening around the country. James Connolly told Nora he had heard that the northerners did not want to fight, but she told him of the Coalisland barn full of armed Volunteers. He then called in the other young women and each of them confirmed what she had said.

When Nora Connolly went to see her father just before he was executed, he told her that if she had not arrived with the news that the northerners were ready to fight, he would not have been able to persuade the rest of the Dublin leaders to go ahead with the Rising.

> My father was lying in bed with a cage over his feet to keep the bedclothes off his shattered ankles. He told us about the court martial, and asked me for news from the North. I had to tell him that the men had gone home, and that there had been no fighting, and I began to cry. But he told me that he was very proud of me.
>
> 'But I've done nothing, nothing,' I said. 'I've just carried messages.'
>
> 'Never mind, Nora,' he said. He told me that if I had not come down with the message from the North that the Northerners were ready to fight, it would not have been possible to persuade the Dublin leaders to go ahead with the Rising. 'Only for you, Nora, we couldn't have done anything,' he told me.[2]

James Connolly had believed that once word got out to the country that the ICA and the Dublin Volunteers under Pearse and MacDonagh were fighting, other areas would join in.

The Belfast women were sent out in pairs, with an ICA man to guide them, to carry the news to each of the members of the Military Council and to summon them to a meeting. Éilis Ní Chorra and her sister Kathleen were taken to see Thomas MacDonagh.

... our guide took us, first of all, to a house on the quays. A very sleepy looking man (when he was satisfied that we were "all right") directed us to another house, and from there we were sent on further to a tall tenement, where Thomas MacDonagh, roused from sleep to hear our account of the activities of the northern Volunteers, was seriously perturbed, declaring that an abortive rising would be fatal, and that MacNeill's demobilisation orders had disorganised everything.[3]

While the other Belfast women were sent to Markievicz's house to sleep, Nora Connolly was kept at Liberty Hall for the meeting of the Military Council, in case she would be needed by them.

Mobilisation in Dublin

That Easter Sunday morning, the full Military Council met in Liberty Hall. Its members were now aware that the mobilisation outside Dublin was a shambles. By 3 p.m. they had made two decisions: first they confirmed the countermand for Sunday; second, they made a new order for the Rising to start at noon on Monday. Messages were sent out around the country.

The women who had been preparing for the mobilisation in Dublin had to cope with this confusion as best they could.

On Saturday night Markievicz had stayed at the home of Jenny Wyse Power, as a precaution against arrest. When she read MacNeill's countermand in the newspaper she rushed to Liberty Hall. Winifred Carney had spent Saturday night there helping to prepare mobilisation orders and officers' commissions. In Liberty Hall ammunition was being handed out.

> On Easter Sunday morning Liberty Hall hummed with activity. Citizen Army men came in with their equipment. Women and girls came along to wish them good luck. For these working class families, dependent on their breadwinners and on their weekly wage, this matter of mobilisation for revolt was a wrenching apart of their hold on life. But there was no repining. They kissed and shook hands, the women handing parcels and boxes of cigarettes.

Women of the Citizen Army Ambulance Unit came in. In one room men and girls were methodically filling the last of the bombs, working up to the last moment to increase the supply of munitions.[4]

The ICA had received mobilisation orders for 3.30 p.m. on Sunday, to coincide with the orders to the Volunteers. When the mobilisation was postponed, most ICA members stayed the night at Liberty Hall, where they organised an impromptu concert. Marie Perolz reported directly to Liberty Hall on her return from Kerry on Sunday night.

Máire Nic Shiubhlaigh's Cumann na mBan Branch had not made plans to participate in the Sunday 'manoeuvres'. Lily O'Brennan had therefore invited Máire to join with her and accompany Eamonn Ceannt's 4th Dublin Battalion. Lily told her to arrive at 3 p.m. with her bicycle. On Easter Sunday, Máire awoke to read the countermand order. Her father, who had some knowledge of the situation in the leadership, advised her to go directly to Lily O'Brennan and confirm whether it was true. Máire and Lily spent the day at the Ceannts' making up first aid kits and assembling equipment for the Volunteers, while Eamonn and Áine spent the day writing and dispatching documents. Nic Shiubhlaigh worked on at the house until about 10 p.m.

That evening, Lily O'Brennan and her sister Áine Ceannt attended eight o'clock Mass. Áine then had an opportunity to explain that a messenger had come for her husband Eamonn during the night and that the day's manoeuvres had been called off. Lily was annoyed, but she did not realise that something more than major manoeuvres had been planned. They returned together to the Ceannt house and from ten o'clock, traffic through the house was so heavy 'we were finally obliged to leave the door ajar — every officer of the Fourth Battalion called to find out what was happening.'[5] Eamonn had left word that all officers were to wait for his return, so 'very soon the garden, from the hall door to the gate, was packed with bicycles. There was such an array of bicycles, it looked as if a whole cycle corps was meeting at the house.'[6]

In the meantime, according to Lily, 'the story of the strange man who had been washed ashore at Banna Strand set us all thinking, and the news of Austin Stack's arrest made us put two and two together".'[7]

Eamonn returned home and instructed all his officers to remain available at their homes. After dinner Lily and Áine went out to gather together all the battalion's dispatch carriers, whilst Eamonn spent the night writing mobilisation orders. Late that night, Lily learned that the mobilisation would take place the next day.

Éilis Ní Rian was on her way home from early Mass with her sister Áine when they got a paper from a newsboy and read of MacNeill's countermand. Later Katy McGuinness, a Lieutenant of the First Battalion, called at Ní Rian's home in North Circular Road, with instructions that the Sunday orders were cancelled, but that she should 'stand to' for further orders. At about 8 p.m. the women went to the Gaelic League office. There they ran into some Volunteers, who like them were looking for information. Everyone was edgy and confused.

May Murray was one of the eighty members of the Inghinidhe branch mobilised at 4 p.m. on Sunday afternoon. (Only two members of the Branch did not manage to turn out.) They were told they should go home, but stay ready. May decided she would spend the evening at a concert, where she heard Brian O'Higgins sing his new song 'The Soldiers of Cumann na mBan' for the first time.

> All honour to Oglaigh na hÉireann
> All praise to the men of our race
> Who, in days of betrayal and slavery
> Saved Ireland from ruin and disgrace
> But do not forget in your praising
> Of them and the deeds they have done
> Their loyal and true-hearted comrades
> The Soldiers of Cumann na mBan

Chorus:
They stand for the honour of Ireland
As their sisters in days that are gone
And they'll march with their brothers to freedom
The Soldiers of Cumann na mBan.

No great-hearted daughter of Ireland
Who died for her sake long ago,
Who stood in the gap of her danger,
Defying the Sassenach foe,
Was ever more gallant or worthy
Of glory in high sounding rann,
Than the comrades of Oglaigh na hÉireann
The soldiers of Cumann na mBan!

O, high beat the hearts of our Mother,
The day she had longed for is nigh,
When the sunlight of joy and of freedom
Shall glow in the eastern sky;
And none shall be honoured more proudly
That morning by chieftain and clan
Than the daughters who served her in danger,
The soldiers of Cumann na mBan!

Nora Foley had returned home after finishing her assignment at Phoenix Park on Saturday to get ready for Sunday's mobilisation. She had been present at the first meeting of Cumann na mBan in Fairview, Dublin the year before. Since then she had taken a course in rifle cleaning and sighting and had studied first aid. When Nora saw the countermand order in the newspaper, she thought it must be a hoax. She went to the Father Mathew Park to link up with the 2nd Battalion of Volunteers as originally instructed. Once there, she learned that there was no hoax.

> Commandant Tom Hunter, O/C Battalion 2, was at the Park and upon hearing my declaration that I refused to go home without orders from 'our own commandant', turned round

and said, 'but I am your commandant; I am in charge of Battalion 2.' I hadn't the heart to tell him I was very well aware of the fact, but it was Cmdt Molly Reynolds [Secretary of Fairview Cumann na mBan] that I referred to.[8]

On being assured that the countermand was only a postponement, she decided there was no point in staying in the park, and returned home.

Confusion in Cork

Ginger O'Connell had arrived in Cork on Good Friday afternoon with MacNeill's countermand, causing confusion and dismay to the leaders there, but Jim Ryan then arrived in the early hours of Saturday with MacNeill's order that the Sunday mobilisation should go ahead. Over 1,000 men — 70 per cent of the brigade — were mobilised by noon on Sunday, but they had very few arms. Because Alice Cashel had been told on Friday night to cancel her transport arrangements, the only vehicle available to the Munster Volunteers was the car belonging to the McDonnells.

On Sunday afternoon, Jim Ryan returned again to Cork, with MacNeill's order, issued late Saturday night, cancelling the Sunday action. The Cork leaders were unaware that the Military Council had met that same afternoon and had issued an order to rise at noon the following day. MacCurtain and MacSwiney set out to demobilise the 1,200 Volunteers who had been mobilised in the Cork area.

At 3 p.m., Sunday, Brigid Foley left Dublin in a taxi for Cork carrying a sealed message from the Military Council, confirming MacNeill's countermand for Sunday and postponing mobilisation until noon Monday. She arrived at 2 a.m., but was unable to evade the police to deliver her message until 11 a.m. on Monday. On arrival at Tomás MacCurtain's house, she was unable to deliver it personally; as instructed, she then destroyed the message and returned to Dublin.

On Sunday night, Pearse gave Marie Perolz a message to carry to Tomás MacCurtain, reiterating that the Rising would start at noon on Monday. Others would carry the same message elsewhere in the country. About 2 a.m. on Monday morning, Perolz went round to the house where Elizabeth O'Farrell and Julia Grenan were sleeping and got them up. Grenan was to deliver the message to Dundalk and Carrickmacross; O'Farrell was to go to Athenry and Galway.

At 7.20 a.m. on Easter Monday, Perolz left Dublin by train to go to Cork, arriving shortly before noon. She took a taxi to MacCurtain's house. Tomás MacCurtain was not there, but when Perolz explained the situation, Mrs MacCurtain sent for Seán MacCurtain, who assured her that 'Cork would do its duty.'[9] Perolz tried to return to Dublin by train, but this was now impossible, so she decided to go to Tralee.

By Monday evening, rumours of action in Dublin had reached Cork, though some said that only the ICA had mobilised. Tomás MacCurtain and Terence MacSwiney arrived back in Cork just before 9 p.m. and were surprised to receive Pearse's new order for a Rising that day. By now, the Cork brigade had spent all day Sunday waiting for orders which never came. They had been demobilised and dispersed and had trudged many miles home, tired, hungry and wet. MacCurtain and MacSwiney decided that it would be irresponsible to try to remobilise with so few arms and when they had lost any advantage of surprise. They decided that a small force would occupy the Volunteer Hall in Cork city and fight if attacked.

Confusion continued to reign throughout the county. Volunteers remained mobilised waiting for orders which did not come; Annie and Mary MacSwiney were kept busy delivering messages back and forth. Some attempts were made to transfer arms out of the city to the country, but the hope of any significant action being taken outside Dublin was lost.

The North and the West

Travelling north on Monday morning with Pearse's urgent message that the Rising would go ahead, Julia Grenan shared the same train as Nora Connolly and Éilis Ní Chorra. They did not acknowledge each other, but when getting off at Dundalk,

Julia whispered, 'I hope the next time we meet it will be in a free Ireland!'[10] Nancy Wyse Power went to Borris, Maeve Cavanagh to Waterford, Elizabeth O'Farrell carried messages for Athenry, Spiddall and Galway. As in Munster, the women found a state of total confusion everywhere.

On Easter Tuesday, Kathleen McDonnell was called to come to Cork to collect her car from the Volunteer Hall. On the way back to Bandon she was briefly arrested. That night the McDonnells' home was raided for the first time.

On Easter Sunday more than 100 men marched from Dingle to Tralee, arriving about 11 a.m.; other men continued to arrive throughout the day. The local Cumann na mBan was waiting with first aid and food.

On Monday Rose Ann Murphy was sent to Dundalk to ask the Volunteers there to join the Rising. She boarded the train at Amiens Street station, but the bridge between Lusk and Rusk had been blown up; the Lord Lieutenant was on the train. Murphy got off the train and walked the remaining forty miles to give the message to the Captain of the Volunteers there, who turned out to be her cousin. Dundalk did turn out, but played only a small part in the Rising.

Action in the South-East

On Thursday, Eily O'Hanrahan had taken Pearse's order, fixing the 23rd as the date for the Rising, to Enniscorthy. (Eily's brother Michael was executed in the aftermath of the Rising.) She was still there when a directive arrived countermanding the order she had brought. The local Volunteers consulted with those of Kilkenny, who were of the opinion that the second order, from MacNeill, was paramount. Séumas Ó Dubhghaill, second lieutenant in Enniscorthy, was sent to Wexford to consult Robert Brennan, Captain of the Wexford Volunteers. After some discussion with Robert and his wife, Una Brennan, it was decided that Ó Dubhghaill should go to Dublin.

In Dublin Sean MacDiarmada told him that MacNeill had decided to fight and showed him an order to Ginger O'Connell to proceed from Cork to Wexford and take command of the Volunteers there. Ó Dubhghaill returned on Friday night and orders for the Sunday manoeuvres were issued. O'Connell arrived on Easter Saturday morning.

MacNeill's countermand sent them into a quandary again. On Easter Monday, Ó Dubhghaill went to Borris with a message for O'Connell. Nancy Wyse Power was there, having brought the Sunday night message from Pearse to go ahead with the insurrection. O'Connell said, 'I suppose we may tell Miss Wyse Power to tell them in Dublin that they will not get any help from this area.'[11] It was decided, however, that a further round of consultations was required. Meanwhile, news came of the Rising in Dublin. Ginger O'Connell returned to Enniscorthy from Borris on Tuesday night with the news that if they rose they would not be supported by the surrounding areas. On Wednesday night, a meeting was held and it was decided nevertheless to seize Enniscorthy the next morning.

Disarray in the West

The plans for the West of Ireland had included seizing military barracks, but the series of orders and countermands left the entire situation in disarray. Elizabeth O'Farrell arrived in Athenry at about 1 p.m. on Easter Monday, carrying Pearse's desperate message, 'We are out from twelve o'clock today. Issue your orders without delay. PHP.'[12] She left the dispatches with Larry Lardner, the Volunteer officer in charge of Athenry. The message she was given in reply was that they would do what they could and Lardner assured her that the messages she brought would be delivered to Galway and Spiddal. Lardner, however, was suspicious because Pearse's signature was not written in full. He believed the ICA was trying to stampede them into a premature insurrection and took no action. Later that afternoon, word came via the Dublin train that the insurrection had begun in the capital. Things then began to move in Athenry and the West.

Elizabeth O'Farrell headed back to Dublin. At Mullingar the train was stopped; this cheered her, because it confirmed that the Rising had indeed begun, but she had to find other means of transport. Eventually she got a lift in a car with a number of other people, for which she was charged two pounds — a significant sum at that time. Back in Dublin that evening, O'Farrell managed to pass through a number of barricades by pretending to be part of a family group. She reported to the General Post Office (GPO), then went home to sleep. On Tuesday morning she was back in the GPO and stayed there until the evacuation.

The plans for Galway, where Liam Mellowes was in charge, were contingent on the arrival of 3,000 guns from the *Aud*. Otherwise, the weaponry at the disposal of the fighters in the area amounted to about 120 rifles and shotguns and a handful of small arms. When news arrived on Easter Monday that the Rising had started in Dublin, Liam Mellowes ordered a mobilisation and more than 1,000 Volunteers turned out. Cumann na mBan also mobilised. Detachments of these Volunteers fought in Oranmore, Clarinbridge and Athenry.

On Thursday they set up headquarters at Moyode Castle. Food was not a problem, as a number of bullocks were seized from the estate of the local gentry. These were slaughtered and made into stew with potatoes and onions from nearby farms. Cumann na mBan did the cooking. Approximately twenty women worked in the camp, providing first aid and other back-up.

The Volunteers in Limerick were involved in the plans for the dispersal of the expected German arms. On Sunday, they received MacNeill's countermand of the Easter Sunday mobilisation from a messenger who arrived by car from Dublin. Pearse's order arrived on Monday, but by then it was too late to mobilise.

Although the Limerick Volunteers were relatively well organised, they had had less than a week's notice of the date of the Rising. Limerick's role was central to the plans for distributing the guns from the *Aud*, and most of the details had to be left to the local leadership to work out. Even at the best of estimates, the Volunteer forces in the area were far below what was needed to carry out Pearse's orders. With the loss of the *Aud* their task was impossible. The Limerick leadership was also acutely aware of the differences between MacNeill and the IRB-led Military Council and attempts were made to clarify the situation.

Limerick received the same series of conflicting orders as did Cork. Volunteers who mobilised on Sunday were sent home. Early on Monday afternoon Agnes and Laura Daly delivered Pearse's message: 'Dublin Brigade goes into action today. Carry out your orders.' The Dalys, who lived in Limerick, were sisters of Edward Daly and Kathleen Clarke. A meeting of the available officers decided that because all their orders depended on the successful landing of the German guns, and because by this time there were only 76 Volunteers left in camp, there was no possibility of joining the fight.

Munster Unable to Fight

Laura Daly and her sister Nora were determined to get to Dublin and join the fight. After some difficulty, they eventually reached the city about 10.30 p.m. Tuesday to find the station occupied by the military. They eventually managed to reach Kathleen Clarke's house in Richmond Avenue. Near midnight, very tired, they arrived at the GPO.

When the Volunteer leaders heard that the Daly sisters had arrived, they decided that as both of them were well known to the leadership in Cork and Limerick, yet another attempt should be made to get those areas to rise. Eamon Dore, of Glin, who himself had come to Dublin for the fight, was asked to escort the sisters back to the station, in that it was hoped there would be a 6.30 a.m. train to Cork and Limerick. The trio left the GPO and went back to the Clarke house, where they rested for a few hours. At daybreak they set out again.

At Mountjoy prison they were stopped at the British military post. Eamon was taken away, and when questioned, said he was taking his two sisters to the station. When he rejoined the two women, he advised them that they should use his name, which they did, being stopped twice more. Laura went on to Limerick, while Nora went to see Tomás MacCurtain and Terence MacSwiney. She spent the night at the MacSwiney house, but by the next morning the Cork leaders had decided that there was no message to send back. Back in Dublin, they went to the GPO to tell Pearse and Connolly the news.

Elizabeth O'Farrell later remembered the impact of the news that Munster would not fight: 'When they came out [from telling Pearse and Connolly] we knew there was bad news from the country. After that we sensed we were losing ground.'[13] Meanwhile, the fires which burned all round the GPO were closing in.

Return to the North

On Easter Sunday morning the six Cumann na mBan members from Belfast had a hurried breakfast at Constance Markievicz's house and then gathered up their kit of water bottles, first aid equipment and haversacks. There was no tram, so they walked to Liberty Hall. They waited in James Connolly's office and eventually he came in carrying a printed copy of the Proclamation. The young women felt honoured to be the first to see it.

James Connolly ordered them to return to the north with a message for the Volunteers. He told them they could not take a copy of the Proclamation as it was too large to dispose of if they were stopped; they memorised it as best they could. The dispatch was hidden in Nell Gordon's hatband, and then they rushed off to the train station. The station was full of soldiers on leave, unaware that the Rising was about to start.

When the women got to Coalisland after many delays, they found that, although all the weapons and much equipment were there, the demobilisation had been completed and there was no one to receive their dispatch. Nora Connolly sent Éilis Ní Chorra to Belfast with the written order and Ina Connolly was sent with a verbal message to Dr MacCartan, a member of the IRB Supreme Council.

The police had been looking for the women at their Coalisland billet, so in the dark and pouring rain the four remaining women were escorted by some local Volunteers to new billets in the countryside. The four were sure that once news of developments in Dublin became known there would be plenty of work for them in Tyrone, but they stayed for almost a week, never straying far from their temporary homes and with little to do but talk to each other. Nora spent the time trying to contact the men who had been demobilised, but was unsuccessful.

4
Dublin Fights

All over Dublin, members of the Volunteers, Fianna Éireann, the Irish Citizen Army and Cumann na mBan were mobilising according to their orders. Many, however, were confused by the countermand and had not turned out. Gradually, as events developed, men and women arrived to join in wherever they could help. The plan drawn up by Joseph Plunkett assumed that at least 9,000 men (and presumably, a proportionate number of women) would turn out, 5,000 of these in Dublin. The plan was to take and hold strategic points in the city and to hold out as long as possible. In the event, only a fraction of that number mobilised. It has been estimated that approximately 1,500–2,500 men actually fought. More than 200 women were mobilised.

Belfast woman Winifred Carney reported to Liberty Hall at 8 a.m. on Monday 14 April 1916. A number of other women were already busy at a cutting machine, cutting up bread and meat rations. At 28 years of age, Winifred was a long-standing campaigner for women's suffrage and a trade union activist. A former secretary of the Textile Workers' Union, in 1916 she was working as James Connolly's secretary. Her first job was to type out the mobilisation orders for the four city battalions of the now unified army of the Irish Republic. (James Connolly had called together the members of the ICA on the eve of the Rising and told them: 'Now there is no more Citizen Army and no more Volunteers, there is only the Army of the Republic.'[1]

By this he meant that all the republican forces were now under the command of the Military Council. It is possible that had things gone differently there would have been a formal merger of the different organisations; what the implications would have been for the status of women in a combined structure can only be surmised.)

At about noon, the Irish Citizen Army formed up outside Liberty Hall in lines of four. The first company to move off, which consisted of about 50 men and a dozen women, marched off across Butts Bridge. After about ten minutes, Sean Connolly's company of about 30, including nine women, marched off towards Dublin Castle. Another group went to the General Post Office. Carney took her place beside James Connolly at the front of this group as it prepared to march off from Liberty Hall for the last time. She was the only woman who took part in the initial occupation of the GPO. Once inside she lost no time in getting settled with her typewriter in front of her and her Webley pistol close at hand. The volunteers were ordered to take their places at the windows and soon Winifred Carney was dealing with her first casualty, a young man who had cut his arm on broken glass.

Molly Reynolds reported first to St Stephen's Green. When she got there she was told that 'the girls were at the Post Office'. She set off with another woman, but on arrival found that Winifred Carney was the only other woman there. Later in the day other Cumann na mBan members arrived and more came in on Tuesday. On Tuesday afternoon, the officers sent away some girls they considered too young to be in the firing line, although girls as young as 14 and 15 years of age were formally attached to the GPO unit. The women set to work organising the kitchen and food stores. Rose Ann Murphy from Liverpool was based in the GPO. Later in the week she helped to carry supplies to the Volunteers occupying Hopkins and Hopkins on Sackville St.

Meanwhile other Cumann na mBan women were bringing in arms and equipment from dumps all over the city and depositing them in the GPO. The women were busy all day going back and forth between the various posts and commands. Other Cumann na mBan members began commandeering food and other supplies. Eventually there were 34 women in the GPO.

May Murray received orders to mobilise on Monday morning. She went to the Walsh home to collect the Walsh sisters, Margaret, Bridie and Mary Jo — all members of Inghinidhe na hÉireann — and reported to Commandant Eily Walsh, remaining with her all day. She worked with Margaret all day Tuesday and Wednesday morning, carrying dispatches. On Tuesday, as they carried ammunition to the GPO, the street they were crossing was swept by rifle fire. By Wednesday afternoon the firing was too heavy for them to go out.

Leslie Price had been a student at the Dominican Training College in Belfast in 1914 and was active in the Gaelic League; in 1915 she went to Dublin for the funeral of O'Donovan Rossa. She joined Cumann na mBan a few days later. About twelve noon on Easter Sunday, an order came telling her to remain at home and wait for instructions. It was 10 a.m. on Monday before she received orders to report at the corner of Blessington Street in an hour's time. As a member of the *Ard Chraobh* branch of Cumann na mBan, she was to be attached to Edward Daly's battalion at the Four Courts. By one o'clock there were still no further instructions, so Leslie and her friend Bríd Dixon decided to go to the GPO. When they arrived there Tom Clarke told them to stay as they could be useful as couriers. At about 4 p.m. Clarke sent Price and Dixon to the outpost at the Hibernian Bank, on the corner of Abbey Street. Price was to take charge of the Cumann na mBan members in the building, and they made tea for the Volunteers there. She remained there almost constantly as the fighting continued. On Wednesday, as she stood beside Tom Weafer, the officer in charge of the post, he was shot and fatally wounded. The post was evacuated shortly afterwards.

After dark each night Price and Dixon carried ammunition and dispatches between the Capuchin Hall and the GPO. They would travel through holes in the walls of buildings as far as Arnott's Department Store, then would have to come out into the street. The second night as they were setting out, Seán MacDiarmada gave them two steel-topped officer's canes, with instructions to use them if anyone tried to touch them. The rapport between men and women, officers and rank and file was very strong. Price remembered later: 'That was the beauty of the men at the time, you could say anything to them.'[2]

On Easter Monday, Louise Gavan Duffy was at her lodgings, working on her MA thesis when someone came and told her the GPO had been taken. (Louise had been a teacher at Pearse's school for girls, St Ita's. She set off to find out for herself what was happening. When she got to the GPO she asked to speak to Pearse. She told him that she believed there was no hope of success and that under the circumstances it was wrong to have started the fight. For this reason, she herself would take no part in the fighting, but if there was a fight, she wanted to be on hand. Pearse accepted this and suggested she work in the kitchen.

This, a big room upstairs, was in the charge of Desmond FitzGerald. Louise was to say later: 'Neither of us was too knowledgeable about cooking or supplying lunches.'[3] Peggy Downey of Liverpool was on hand, however, and she was more sure of herself. She assessed the stocks and advised that with great care the food could last two or three weeks. This news was passed on to Pearse, who responded, 'Be very careful with it then, because who knows how long we'll be needing it for.'[4] This order was taken very seriously; May Murray was later stopped by FitzGerald as she was taking soup and a slice of bread to one of the men and told to divide the bread between two.

Despite the apparent optimism of Pearse's words, all the republican forces expected to be crushed; by common consent, though, it was to be a fight to the finish. They hoped to hold out two or three weeks, long enough to be able to draw international attention to the cause of the nation. The leadership's strategy was to establish that they represented the sovereign forces of the Irish people, at war with England. As recognised combatants, they would have grounds to insist on representation at the post-war peace negotiations. The insurgents therefore tried to comply with international conventions such as the wearing of uniforms by combatants and the treatment of prisoners. The British forces on the other hand often disregarded even the Red Cross symbol.

City Hall

As soon as the Rising began, Constance Markievicz went out with Kathleen Lynn to deliver medical supplies.

> I went off then with the Doctor in her car. We carried a large store of first aid necessities and drove off through quiet dusty streets and across the river, reaching the City Hall just at the very moment that Commandant Sean Connolly and his little troop of men and women swung around the corner and he raised his gun and shot the policeman who barred the way. A wild excitement ensued, people running from every side to see what was up. The Doctor got out, and I remember Mrs Barrett — sister of Sean Connolly — and others helping to carry in the Doctor's bundles.[5]

Markievicz was later rumoured to have killed the unarmed Constable Lahiff at St Stephen's Green at around noon on Monday. In fact she was at the time delivering supplies with Dr Lynn and only arrived at the Green later in the afternoon. She did take part in the fighting later that day when a party of Royal Irish Rifles came along Camden Street. She joined in holding them off and also took part in sniping from the roof of the College of Surgeons.

Dr Lynn's orders were to stay with Sean Connolly's City Hall contingent. When she arrived, the iron gates were shut, so she had to scramble over them to get in. The City Hall group consisted of 16 men and nine women (at times there may have been 11 women here.) Emily and Annie Norgrove were part of this garrison and Molly O'Reilly acted as courier. The group's first objective had been Dublin Castle. The policeman on guard attempted to stop them and Sean Connolly shot him. Connolly ordered his force to go in, but they hesitated, and a soldier shut the gate. Helena Molony fired a shot at this point to warn the soldier off and one man hurled a bomb at the guardroom window, but it failed to explode. Sean Connolly decided not to attempt a further attack on the Castle. It was assumed that the

Castle would be well fortified and the republicans had now lost the advantage of surprise. In fact there were only 10 soldiers and a few RIC men in the Castle at the time.

The contingent decided to take the City Hall and the *Evening Mail* offices instead. Sean Connolly, shot raising the Tricolour over the City Hall, was the first republican casualty. By the time Kathleen Lynn crawled across the roof to where Helena Molony cradled his head in her lap, he was dead.

Helena Molony and Molly O'Reilly were sent to the GPO to ask for reinforcements, but there were none to send. They came back with the orders to hang on as long as possible. Helena was in charge of food at the City Hall. She managed to find some oatmeal and made porridge.

At one point on Monday afternoon, Dr Lynn and Helena Molony, the senior officers of the garrison, were considering evacuating the City Hall. They looked out the window and saw what appeared to be rain or sleet — it was a torrent of bullets. Helena took a prisoner — a British soldier — who was held at City Hall. In the evening the fighting at the City Hall and *Evening Mail* intensified; the shelling by British forces was intense. Helena expected that the place would collapse around them at any time, so heavy was the machine gun fire.

At about 6 p.m. Matt Connolly, younger brother of Katie Barrett and Sean Connolly, was called down from the roof of the City Hall and examined by Dr Lynn. She used the opportunity to tell the fifteen-year-old of Sean's last moments and of the work Katie was doing as a nurse. Matt had not slept for three days and was sent to a small room to get some rest. When he woke some hours later, 'the building seemed to shudder and vibrate with explosions and machine gun fire. Glass crashed, doors and woodwork were being shattered, and somewhere in the distant part of the building a woman screamed.'[6]

Under cover of night, British soldiers attacked the City Hall, coming in over the roofs of neighbouring buildings. Matt Connolly later recalled:

As the afternoon wore on and dusk was falling, the troops
assembled in passages and shelters around the upper yard
[of the Castle] in preparation for a massed attack on the City
Hall garrison which had caused them heavy losses during
the day. One member of the garrison, a woman, on sentry
duty on the ground floor at the time has told us '...There was
a large window on the ground floor. On this they
concentrated. They bombed and blasted it with machine gun
fire. The din was terrific, the effect nerve-shattering. Bullets
and bursting grenades smashed into and exploded on the
ground floor.' Behind the pillars the woman and a wounded
man took what shelter they could. Some of the men had
come down from the roof to try to stem the tide, but in vain.[7]

After dark, soldiers with fixed bayonets charged through the
hole they had made in the back wall.

A British officer flashed a torch and called out for whoever
was in charge. Doctor Lynn stepped forward. He called on
her to surrender. She had no choice, so she obeyed and the
ground floor group, consisting mostly of women, were taken
prisoners. Soldiers dashed upstairs opening doors and firing
into rooms as they went. One of the most remarkable things
about this whole attack is the small number of casualties
among the garrison of the City Hall. Another is that the
soldiers did not attempt to get to the roof where all the firing
had come from during the day.[8]

An incident recounted by Jenny Shanahan perhaps explains
why the soldiers did not attempt to reach the roof until some
hours later. The soldiers went up the stairs and came upon
Shanahan, who they took to be a civilian. The officer demanded,
'Have they treated you badly?' 'Oh no, sir,' said she, falling
swiftly into her new role. 'They have treated me well enough,
but there must be hundreds of them up there on the roof!'[9]
At Ship Street barracks, the women who had been captured
were held in a room containing offensive-smelling rubbish bins
until, at Dr Lynn's insistence, the bins were removed.
Unfortunately, Jenny Shanahan's status as a civilian was short-
lived. She was brought to Ship Street Barracks, where the other
women of her garrison welcomed her warmly. Her captor's
disgusted response was, 'Oh, so you're one of them, are you?'[10]

Dr Lynn and Helena Molony were taken to Dublin Castle. 'Miss Molony was discovered a few hours later with the lock half off her door, her fingers bleeding pitifully from attempts to get out.'[11]

The group in the *Evening Mail* office held out until Tuesday evening. The *Irish Times* reported that 26 dead were found there.

St. Stephen's Green

Most of the 138-strong St Stephen's Green contingent were ICA members, including about 15 women. They were under the direction of Commandant Mallin. Constance Markievicz, second-lieutenant in the ICA, was designated his second-in-command. She wrote later:

> When I reported with the car to Commandant Mallin in Stephen's Green, he told me that he must keep me. He said that owing to MacNeill's calling off the Volunteers, a lot of the men who should have been under him had had to be distributed round other posts, and that few of those left him were trained to shoot, so I must stay and be ready to take up the work of a sniper. He took me round the Green and showed me how the barricading of the gates and digging trenches had begun, and he left me in charge of this work while he went to superintend the erection of barricades in the streets and arrange other work. About two hours later he definitely promoted me to be his second-in-command. This work was very exciting as the fighting began. I continued round and round the Green, reporting back if anything was wanted, or tackling any sniper who was particularly objectionable.[12]

The ambiguous attitude of some of the men to the involvement of their women comrades is revealed in the written account by Frank Robbins. Noting that only a fraction of the expected men had answered the mobilisation order, he observed: 'Mallin had actually to avail of the services of members of the Women's Section of the Citizen Army to guard the gates of St Stephen's Green and to eject citizens who were inside the Green when the takeover began. Madame Markievicz, Lily Kempson and Mary Hyland gave invaluable service.'[13] Although he acknowledged the contribution of the women, Robbins seems to have had some difficulty in accepting the policy of no distinctions between men and women within the ICA. At one point during the week, Madeleine ffrench-Mullen threatened him with arrest and court-martial over a dispute about her order that he drink spirits for medicinal purposes. The situation was only resolved when Markievicz was called upon to intervene and accepted his argument that as a teatotaller, he had a conscientious objection to drinking alcohol.

When Nora Foley arrived at Stephen's Green, she expected to join the Second Battalion of Volunteers, but it was not there. She was nevertheless given a warm welcome by Constance Markievicz and Madeleine ffrench-Mullen, who was organising a first aid post in the summerhouse and concerned that there were not enough first aid workers. Bridie Gough entertained them all with jokes as they worked. Rosie Hackett, May Moore and Bridget Murtagh made up the rest of the first aid team, and Nell Gifford was in charge of the commissariat. Her staff were Molly Hyland and Kate Kelly.

Margaret Skinnider was detailed as a dispatch rider for the St. Stephen's Green command and was sent out to scout the city.

> If I did not find the military moving I was to remain at the end of the Green until I should see our men coming in to take possession. There were no soldiers in sight; only a policeman standing at the end of the Green. He paid no attention to me; I was only a girl on a bicycle. But I watched him closely.[14]

She toured the city, then carried a dispatch from Mallin to the GPO and returned with the reply.

> As soon as I returned I was sent away again to bring in sixteen men guarding Leeson Street Bridge. If we abandoned the Green before they could join us they would be cut off. As I rode along on my bicycle I had my first taste of being under fire. Bullets struck the rim of my bicycle wheels and rattled among the spokes. I knew one might hit me at any moment, but speed saved my life and I was soon out of range around the corner of Leeson Street. As I reached this

group and transmitted the order for their return, I scouted ahead up the streets I knew would bring us back safely to the College, unless already guarded by the British. At another spot a woman leaned out of her window just as I was passing. 'You are losing your gun,' she called to me. My revolver had torn its way through the pocket of my raincoat ...

Every time I left the College I was forced to run the gauntlet of this machine gun fire, and I blessed the enemy's bad markmanship several times a day. Once that day I saw them shooting at our first aid girls, who made excellent targets in their white dresses with large red crosses on them. It was a miracle that none of them was wounded. Bullets passed through one girl's skirt, and another had the heel of her shoe shot off.[15]

That night the republicans slept out in the Green. It was damp and cold. The women slept on the benches in the summerhouse, which although it had no walls, did at least have a roof.

Boland's Mills

The Boland's Mills garrison was under the command of Eamon de Valera. His Third Battalion of the Dublin Brigade of the Irish Volunteers was to have a complement of 400, but because of MacNeill's countermand there were only 120. 'The Commandant and his staff were driven to the end of their ingenuity to compensate for their lack of numbers,' one of his men tells us.[16] Apparently their ingenuity did not stretch too far. A detachment of Cumann na mBan were mobilised to give them assistance, but after they had waited an hour and a half, a cyclist was sent to tell them they could go home. De Valera refused to have women attached to his unit and Boland's Mills was the only garrison which did not have women assigned to it.

Commandant Joseph O'Connor gives a coy explanation for the absence of women in this garrison.

It was arranged that as the units were marching into their positions Cumann na mBan, who had paraded at Merrion Square, should join with the Companies and enter the bakery with 'C' Company, from whence they would operate. Unfortunately the arrangement fell through. I think it was the fact of remaining so long at Earlsfort Terrace that made us anxious to reach our positions before twelve o'clock. This is the explanation of how we were deprived of the assistance of Cumann na mBan.[17]

George Lyons was more forthright about what happened.

There was no ambulance service attached to the Third Battalion during Easter Week. De Valera, largely I believe, at the instigation of one who was notoriously 'girl-shy', failed to send the promised courier to the local Cumann na mBan, who were mobilised on Merrion Square awaiting his instructions. He decided that they would probably be an encumbrance where an extremely mobile force was necessary, and that anyhow women should be spared, as far as possible, from witnessing the horrors of war, especially the class of war we expected to develop.[18]

A number of these women made their way to Jacob's factory, where they were welcomed.

South Dublin

The south Dublin area was the responsibility of Eamonn Ceannt and the Fourth Battalion. Ceannt based his forces in the South Dublin Union, with outposts in the Marrowbone Distillery, Watkin's Brewery, Roe's Distillery and Mount Brown. His forces consisted of approximately 50 men and 26 women.

Part of the Inghinidhe branch of Cumann na mBan was attached to Ceannt's Fourth Battalion. Lily O'Brennan had been advised to link up with them because the confusion caused by the countermand would make it difficult for her to tie in with her own group. Still under the impression that they were to be engaged in manoeuvres, after breakfast on Easter Monday, she packed a day's rations into her nephew's schoolbag, along with her water bottle, a first aid kit, soap, towel and comb, her prayerbook, a notebook and pencil. Like most of the women she did not have a uniform, so she was dressed in the sturdy clothes she wore for hillwalking. She set off by bicycle for her 10.30 a.m. rendezvous.

Soon the order came to fall in. Her unit was in charge of a horse and cart full of ammunition. She assumed they were heading for Phoenix Park and even now still under the impression they were engaged in manoeuvres, thought, 'fighting will probably occur and we will have to retreat to the Dublin mountains'.[19] Eventually they arrived in Marrowbone Lane.

> I heard a knock. It was the butt-end of a rifle on the high wooden gates. Then rang out the clear commanding order from the captain in charge of our unit: 'Open in the name of the Irish Republic'.
>
> A wicket door was opened. There was a little parley and delay, but Captain Séumas Ó Murchada and his guard forced their way in. The big gates flew open and the Volunteers and Cumann na mBan filed into the courtyard, the horse and cart rumbled quickly over its cobblestones; then the gates were quickly closed, and army manouevres at once began ...
>
> I knew, now, that we had thrown down the gauntlet to the British Empire and that, placing our trust in God, we looked for victory.[20]

The South Dublin Union was of particular strategic importance because of its location, near the Richmond and Island Bridge barracks, Kingsbridge railway terminus and the Royal Hospital, which was the British military headquarters for Ireland. In total it covered approximately fifty acres and had the appearance of a good-sized town. In Easter week it was the scene of heavy fighting, including a number of hand-to-hand battles. Yet during the course of the week the 3,282 inmates and the officials who cared for them remained, although inmates were removed from some of the more dangerous buildings. Red Cross flags were hung on all the buildings not occupied by Volunteers. A civilian nurse, Margaretta Keogh, was killed here. (A plaque commemorating Nurse Keogh is to be found inside Baggot Street Hospital.)

> The six Volunteers on the top floor of Hospital No. 2-3 had withdrawn, as stated, to the east side of the building. On the same floor, on the west side, Nurse Keogh and another nurse congratulated themselves on the fact that the military were not attacking the building. 'Thank God', said Nurse Keogh to her companion, "there will be no bloodshed here." Suddenly, however, shots rang out beneath them — the volley fired on the two Volunteers escaping from the ground

floor. Nurse Keogh immediately decided to look after the safety of the inmates on the lower floor. As she descended the long stone stairway leading to the ground floor on her errand of mercy, she was shot dead.

At the foot of the stairs a porch and door open at right angles into the side of a long corridor. This corridor was occupied by the military; and two soldiers kneeling back, out of sight, covered the open doorway with their rifles. Immediately the nurse's white linen uniform flashed before them, as she entered the corridor, they fired, both shots entering her body and killing her instantly.

Her companion then rushed down. As she entered, she heard an officer shout: 'Are there any Sinn Feiners upstairs?'[21]

The National Graves Association account differs in that it says that Nurse Keogh went to the assistance of an injured Volunteer and that as she bent over the wounded man, she herself was fired upon and killed. Their tribute to Nurse Keogh noted that, 'Eamonn Ceannt addressed the men afterwards, and declared that Nurse Keogh was the First Martyr and asked the Volunteers to so remember her. This account of her heroic death is inserted at the request of the Garrison of the South Dublin Union ...'[22]

Marrowbone Lane

The women who camped at Marrowbone Lane stayed until the surrender the following Sunday. Marrowbone was under the charge of Con Colbert, who had been one of Markievicz's 'Fianna boys'. All the women were trained in first aid and they were also responsible for procuring and preparing food. Mary Byrne and Margaret Kennedy (later a Senator) were also among the women attached to Ceannt's battalion.

The women were given hand grenades made from milk tins to drop over the bridge onto the roadway in case of attack. Food was requisitioned and bread and milk were commandeered. The latter came in the form of a cow with two calves. One of the calves was killed. The women made soda bread and even butter, and this unit at least had plenty of milk and buttermilk. Sympathetic local women brought the garrison jugs of hot tea in the mornings. Not all the locals were friendly, however. A detail going out to find stretchers was confronted by a group of pro-British women.

Men and women alike slept on straw and sacks, but despite the fairly primitive conditions, morale in this garrison was extremely high. A tunnel was dug and the women were told they could use it for escape if need be. They were not impressed. 'What do you think we came here for?' asked one.[23] As it turned out, the tunnel was later discovered to end in a policeman's house! On the Thursday, this garrison saw some of the fiercest fighting of the Rising, when they experienced an attack by over 500 British troops.

Jacob's Factory

On Easter Monday morning the actress Máire Nic Shiubhlaigh was at 10 o'clock Mass when her father came to the church with a telegram from Lily O'Brennan. She immediately went home and changed into her Cumann na mBan uniform and took a tram into the city. At the College of Surgeons she met a body of Volunteers and saw Thomas MacDonagh and Joseph Plunkett there. She collected her bicycle from a house in South Richmond Street and cycled to Ceannt's house in Dolphin's Barn. The house was empty and only then did she realise that she had no idea where they had gone. 'The silent house was puzzling. Though Eamonn and Lily had gone on a route march, someone should have been left behind. Yet, even then the possibility of a rising never struck me.'[24]

Near Wellington Barracks a British army car forced her bicycle into the kerb and she came off. A British officer got out of the car and apologised, as Máire pulled her coat around her uniform. He put her bicycle on the luggage rack of the car and offered her a lift. She refused; he then offered to take her to a doctor. Máire removed her bike from the car and limped away; he followed slowly in the car. Finally in desperation, she got on the bike and cycled until he left her. Then, in much pain, she got off the bike. She stopped at the home of a dentist friend, who saw the leg and assumed she had been shot. It was then that she heard shooting nearby and realised that the Volunteers had been mobilised.

She then went to see Mrs O'Keeffe, an officer in Cumann na mBan and sister-in-law of Jenny Wyse Power, who had a shop in Camden Street. Mrs O'Keeffe sent her to the Sinn Féin office at 6 Harcourt Street, where Sara Kealy, Kathleen Lane, Annie McQuade and the Pollard sisters were waiting for orders. A man came by and told them that the ICA was taking St. Stephen's Green and the Volunteers were taking Jacob's. Sara had already been to Jacob's, so it was decided they would go there. On the way they were confronted by an angry crowd of Jacob's workers and 'Separation Allowance' women. (These were wives of British soldiers who were in receipt of government payments because their husbands were overseas.)

Arriving at Jacob's, they met Thomas MacDonagh, who was concerned because no provision had been made for women. Unlike de Valera, however, he valued their offer to cook and tend casualties. The women returned briefly to Harcourt Street looking for reinforcements, but no one was there. They returned to Jacob's at about 12.45 and arranged the storage of equipment. Jacob's was being secured. There were approximately 130-150 men, some Fianna and the Cumann na mBan women in the garrison. MacDonagh came in and read the Proclamation to the assembled men and women and the republican flag was hoisted over the factory.

All gas and electricity had been shut off for safety reasons, so they used a small forge for their kitchen.

> [W]e found a perfectly-equipped but useless kitchen, formerly equipped with gas and electricity. Three Volunteers disconnected a couple of immense copper boilers and carried them down to the forge where we set them on the fire. They made excellent urns for boiling meat and vegetables and brewing tea. Despite constant foraging the first day no food suitable for hungry men could be found. There were biscuits in plenty — 'plain and fancy' — mostly fancy — slabs of rich fruit cake, some shortbread, and a few tons of cream crackers. But there was nothing of which to make a hot

drink. Eventually one of the girls found a gross or two of slab cooking chocolate. It was grated into the biggest boiler and stewed until it melted. The result was a dark brown cocoa-like syrup, taken without sugar or milk. It looked horrible, but at least it was sustaining.[25]

As the senior member of Cumann na mBan there, Máire Nic Shiubhlaigh was in charge of the women and reported to the Volunteer staff. The women stayed in the bottom of the factory and were ordered not to go upstairs unescorted. They were thus cut off from events outside, but this order was relaxed later in the week.

Reis' Chambers and Father Mathew Hall

Éilis Ní Rian was on her way home from Mass on Easter Sunday when she read MacNeill's countermand in a newspaper. Later on in the morning, she was visited by Katy McGuinness, a lieutenant of the First Battalion, who ordered her to 'stand to'. By 8 p.m., when she had still received no further news, she went to the Gaelic League offices on North Frederick Street where she found some other men and women volunteers, but still failed to obtain any real information.

Early on Easter Monday morning, Ní Rian received orders to collect other Cumann na mBan members and report with full kit. By the time she had collected stretchers and called for her comrades, it was noon when she arrived at Palmerston Place near the Black Church, where she waited with Eileen Parker, Emily Elliott and others for the rest of the day. They heard shooting, but were given no work to do. At 6 p.m. a cyclist came with a dispatch telling them to go home.

Ní Rian was a member of the Ard Craobh branch of Cumann na mBan. Emily Elliott came from a republican family and was herself a founder member of the organisation. In 1914 she had been an apprentice confectioner at Hughes Brothers in Ranelagh, and she later worked in various confectionery establishments.

Éilis Ní Rian and Emily Elliott decided to go to the GPO and volunteer their services. The sentry on duty there told them they were not needed in the GPO, but he suggested they try

Reis' Chambers across the street. James Connolly had sent a number of Volunteers to take over what had formerly been a wireless school. They were busy trying to repair equipment left there and make contact with the outside world on behalf of the Irish Republic. The young women found they were very welcome, but there was no food and no cooking facilities at the outpost.

On Tuesday at daylight they set out together to cross Sackville Street [now O'Connell Street], which was by now a mass of barbed wire and barricades. They eventually negotiated the distance to the GPO and after careful interrogation, they were allowed in to see Desmond FitzGerald, quartermaster of the GPO garrison. When they requested food for the Volunteers in Reis' Chambers, FitzGerald said he could not give it to them without a written order from the officer in charge of the outpost. It took some time for the women to convince him of the difficulties they had encountered there and that they could not return without food for the hungry Volunteers. After returning and organising the meal, the women decided to go in search of Emily's sister, Éilis. Along the way they delivered some dispatches.

When they returned to Reis' Chambers, they were told that word had come that Cumann na mBan members were needed at the Four Courts, and they set off once again, winding their way through back streets to avoid shooting. On arrival they were directed to the Father Mathew Hall, where they were welcomed by one of the priests. The Hall had been taken over as a hospital on Tuesday.

A number of Cumann na mBan members from different branches were already present there: Mrs Fahy, Mrs Conlon and Katy McGuinness had husbands who were operating nearby. Mrs Murphy was a member of Inghinidhe na hÉireann. Margaret Martin, Lily Murnane, Dora Hartford and Kathleen Martin were all members of the Columcille branch. (In 1916 there were three branches of Cumann na mBan in Dublin: Central, with headquarters at 25 Parnell Square, Inghinidhe na hÉireann, based at 6 Harcourt Street, and Columcill, in Blackhall

Place). Also present were Christina Hayes, Eileen Parker, Kathleen Kenny and Eileen Walsh. All were given armbands and orders through the senior members of their own branch. In the early days at least the male Volunteers kept the hospital well supplied with food — ham, tomatoes, milk, sugar and tea. Éilis Ní Rian ate tomatoes here for the first time in her life.

For the first few days they helped in the kitchen. At first most of the injuries were minor, but as the week went on the number of serious injuries increased. The women with first aid training were transferred to work in the Father Mathew Hall, which was full of beds. They continued performing first aid duties and delivering food to the barricades until Friday. Éilis Ní Rian recalled that one of the barricades had a cab in the middle of it, and it was necessary to open the doors and climb through it to get out the other side. There was very fierce fighting in this area for much of the week.

On Thursday morning, some of the women from the Father Mathew Hall went round to visit their comrades at the Four Courts. Katy McGuinness and Mrs Morkan were already travelling back and forth between the posts as part of their duties. The Four Courts garrison included sisters Mollie and Dolly O'Sullivan, Pauline Morkan, Nellie Ennis, Máire Carron, Brighid Lyons, Rose McGuinness, Carrie Mitchell and Maggie Derham. Derham had met Áine Ní Rian at their digs on Tuesday and they had gone together to the GPO. Maggie had volunteered to work at the Four Courts because her brother was a Volunteer in the area. They then went round to visit some of the men on the barricades. The women would not see some of them again until their return from prison.

As fighting intensified, it became more difficult for the women to leave the makeshift hospital and the men themselves brought in their wounded comrades. The most seriously wounded were taken directly to Richmond Hospital.

College of Surgeons

On Tuesday, the republican force led by Mallin and Markievicz was obliged to fall back to the College of Surgeons. About 3 p.m. it was decided that it would not be possible to hold St. Stephen's Green and an evacuation was ordered.

The Red Cross post on St. Stephen's Green had come under fire. The women had to drag their casualties through the bushes to the College of Surgeons. In the confusion Chris Caffrey and Rosie Hackett were nearly left behind. They had to take shelter in the caretaker's house, then make a run for it. Joe Connolly had to hold a hostile mob at bay while the women ducked and ran. A man close behind them was shot dead by snipers just as he reached the door.

Frank Robbins was assigned to lead the takeover of the College of Surgeons. It was believed that there was a stock of British arms in the building. Mallin assigned Markievicz, Mary Hyland, Lily Kempson and another woman to the group, along with three men. 'On finding the arms the women were to transport them back to Stephen's Green. I was to occupy the College and remain there with my three men.'[26] No arms were found initially and the women reported back to Mallin. But later Markievicz had more luck when she discovered 67 rifles, 15,000 rounds of ammunition and a supply of bandoliers and haversacks. The College of Surgeons then became the republican headquarters for the St. Stephen's Green area.

On the third floor they found a kitchen. Nellie Gifford, a trained cook who had given lessons at Liberty Hall on camp and emergency cooking, was put in charge and ran the operation professionally, as the *Irish Times* later reported.

> Down in the kitchen large quantities of canned foods and provisions of every description were discovered in orderly array. Some sort of discipline seems to have been maintained in the commissariat department. A slate was discovered on which was inscribed: 'IRA orderly for this kitchen Miss —. In her absence — .'[27]

This description of plenty notwithstanding, lack of food was in fact a pressing problem here. At one point, Lily Kempson held up a bread cart at gunpoint and Mary Hyland comandeered a milk float by similar means. Constance Markievicz recalled: 'Some of the girls had revolvers, and with these they sallied forth and held up bread vans.'[28] Nell took rations round to the men in the houses around St. Stephen's Green. It was a difficult and dangerous task to deliver food to the various outposts. 'As each house was taken it had to be guarded and this meant that food had to be carried under fire past the lane beside the College and through rough holes in walls where a bullet through the windows on the landings threatened us as we clambered up assisted by the men on guard in these lonely houses.'[29] On her return she took with her supplies of brandy and food commandeered from the houses.

Food

In many of the garrisons, food was a serious problem throughout the week. Before the women could cook the food, very often they would have to scavenge for it, or commandeer it from not always co-operative sources. Sometimes the women bringing food into the garrison were taken to be looters and this sometimes helped to protect them from the unsympathetic crowds. Despite the women's best efforts, many republicans were fighting on empty stomachs. Hanna Sheehy-Skeffington spent the early part of the week delivering food supplies to various garrisons. Later in the week sympathetic citizens brought food to some of the insurgent posts. Chris Caffrey risked her life several times during the week carrying messages between St. Stephen's Green and the GPO and searching for food. Later in the week sacks of potatoes came in from supporters in the country. The Liverpool and Cork branches of Cumann na mBan sent food parcels.

Lack of food was already a major problem at St. Stephen's Green by Tuesday. There were few delivery vans which could be taken over and the numbers of republicans concentrated in the College of Surgeons had greatly increased. Constance Markievicz recalled:

> Nellie Gifford was put in charge of one large classroom with a big grate, but alas, there was nothing to cook. When we were all starving she produced a quantity of oatmeal from somewhere and made pot after pot of the most delicious

porridge, which kept us going. But all the same, on Tuesday and Wednesday we absolutely starved. There seemed to be no bread in the town. Later on Mary Hyland was given charge of a little kitchen, somewhere down through the houses...[30]

Towards midnight on Wednesday Liam Ó Briain was sent to get food for his comrades.

I went to the back of the darkened building and met Miss Nellie Gifford who had been slaving away in the kitchen all the week. Her sister, Mrs Thomas MacDonagh, was to be widowed a few days later. 'There are fourteen of us who have had nothing since Tuesday,' I said. She managed to get me a biscuit tin full of boiled rice. I didn't blame her, she could not give me what she hadn't got. I came back in triumph with my biscuit tin. At least the rice was hot. We all gathered round and there was about a ladle-full for each man.[31]

Early in the week Chris Caffrey and Nell Gifford went to Jacob's to arrange for some flour to be sent over to the College of Surgeons. A rumour that there was plenty of food at the GPO sent them over there on Tuesday morning. The GPO indeed had considerable quantities of bread, milk and beef commandeered from the hotels nearby. The two women took a considerable supply and were standing outside the GPO, wondering how to get their load back, when Francis Sheehy-Skeffington came along. When they explained their predicament, he called two newsboys over and gave them money to carry the food back to the College of Surgeons. This was probably the last recorded act of Sheehy-Skeffington before his arrest and murder by the British. (The officer responsible was later acquitted by a court martial by reason of insanity.)

Food supplies and information about troop movements were not the only sort of help volunteered by sympathetic citizens. On Tuesday, during heavy firing, a woman in a nurse's uniform arrived at the outpost next to the Imperial Hotel and insisted on coming into the building. Eventually a ladder was dropped down and she was dragged through the window. She stayed and helped to nurse the wounded until the evacuation. It is likely that it was this woman who later wrote her account as an anonymous Red Cross Nurse:

> Many of the women were snipers, and both in the Post Office
> and in the Imperial Hotel the present writer, who was a Red
> Cross nurse, saw women on guard with rifles, relieving
> worn-out Volunteers ... These women could throw hand
> grenades, they understood the use of bombs; in fact, they
> seemed to understand as much about the business of warfare
> as their men.[32]

On Tuesday Julia Grenan and Elizabeth O'Farrell took the
copy for *War News* to the printer (only one issue of this
broadsheet was printed during Easter Week). They went on to
deliver some of the posters to MacDonagh and Jacob's, running
the gauntlet of British snipers on the way. When they got back
to the GPO, they were told that St. Stephen's Green had sent
over for ammunition and food. They set out yet again, this time
accompanied by 14 year old May McLoughlin. The three of
them were packed around with .303 ammunition. Before they
left, James Connolly gave them some money and told them to
buy food with it.

At the corner of George's Street and Dame Street the way
was lined by soldiers. Grenan told young May McLoughlin to
run across the road and if she was stopped, to say she was
looking for her brother. She managed to pass, but a soldier
stopped Grenan and O'Farrell, telling them it was too dangerous
for them to go further. Grenan asked him if there were soldiers
up George's Street. Just as he was confirming that there were,
Grenan felt something heavy strike her leg. It was a round of
ammunition slipping down. She leaned against the wall, trying
to ascertain what was wrong, when the soldier offered to see
them to safety. He escorted them to the top of George's Street
and they thanked him warmly.

They were welcomed at the College of Surgeons. Suddenly,
Markievicz was called to deal with a sniper on the church. She
returned shortly, saying, 'I got that sniper!'[33] Grenan,
McLoughlin and O'Farrell then went to a shop in York Street
run by a member of Clan na Gael and bought two dozen loaves
of bread and some cheese. The shopkeeper offered to deliver
the food to the garrison. In York Street, they met some other
women who told them of being attacked by a group of pro-

British women. They had been rescued by a priest, who had told the attackers that they should not interfere in a military conflict between one country and another.

Grenan, McLoughlin and O'Farrell returned to the GPO, passing Liberty Hall, which was lined with sandbags. Soon after, Joe McGuinness gave them a dispatch to deliver to the Four Courts, saying, 'For God's sake, don't let it be captured.'[34] It contained the plan for blowing up the Linen Hall Barracks. James Connolly later came to Julia Grennan and said, 'Well, they obeyed your orders.' 'What orders?' asked the surprised Julia. 'The ones that you gave them at the Four Courts.' 'I didn't give them any orders,' said Julia. 'Didn't you carry a dispatch telling them to blow up the Linen Hall!,' he said.[35]

Dangerous Missions

Michael Mallin decided that it would be necessary to send a small party out to rush the United Services Club, from which there was fierce enemy sniping. Most of the men at the College of Surgeons had had no sleep since Sunday, but after a rest, a group left with Constance Markievicz as their guide. They had to go over a plank stretched across a thirty-foot drop between the College of Surgeons and the roof of the Turkish baths alongside. Most of them, including Markievicz, went across on hands and knees.

Madeleine ffrench-Mullen on Wednesday announced to the women in the College of Surgeons that anyone who wished could go home. Thinking that this meant things were going so well outside they were being allowed leave to visit their families, Nora Foley immediately said she would go. She changed her mind rapidly when it became clear that they were being offered a last chance to get away safely.

On Wednesday also, Pearse sent for Julia Grenan. 'I want you to do a very dangerous mission. This is a letter to the British and you'll have to go to the British lines with it. I don't mind if you refuse.' 'Well, I came to do what I'm asked to do, and I'm doing that,' Grenan replied.[36]

The British had burned down a Red Cross unit near Clery's. Pearse's message to the British was that if another incident of this sort took place something would happen to some of the British hostages. Grenan asked that her friend Elizabeth O'Farrell be allowed to go with her and they set off together in search of the British lines.

> In Parliament Street, near Capel Street Bridge, they came into the line of fire. Holding the letter above her head, Miss O'Farrell advanced, her friend beside her. Bullets hopped along the pavement by their feet and struck the brickwork of the walls. Soldiers screamed at them to go back but they advanced steadily. From the Sunlight Soap building, a big building on the quays, firing was continuous, but the girls walked through it.
>
> They walked right up to the line of soldiers across Dame Street and Eustace Street. One excited soldier rushed out of the ranks and held his bayonet to Miss O'Farrell's breasts. She still held her letter aloft. An officer, with a revolver strapped to each wrist, came dashing up. Miss Grenan snatched the letter from her friend and handed it to the officer. The audacity of the whole proceeding left the soldiers speechless and the women were able to walk away without any cross-examination.[37]

On their return they were fired on from the Customs House as they crossed the Bridge. Later, when James Connolly was wounded, he told Julia Grenan: 'When I was lying there in the lane I thought of how often you two went up and down there and nothing ever happened yez!'[38]

Linda Kearns opened a Red Cross field hospital near North Great Georges Street, collecting bedding from nearby houses. She had six girls and two boys to assist her. Their first patients included several women, some republican soldiers and a British soldier whose fingers had been shot off.

One night, at midnight, Nell Gifford and Chris Caffrey, one of the workers at the Liberty Hall shirt-makers' co-operative, were sent from the College of Surgeons to Jacob's for ammunition. The factory was surrounded by an friendly crowd of Separation Allowance women, and they had to be lifted in through a window. On the way out they were attacked by the crowd. But Chris, who had risked her life many times carrying messages from the College of Surgeons to the GPO and Jacob's, was to have an even more harrowing experience.

On Wednesday, Mallin had sent her to the GPO, but she had failed to get through; she returned in an extremely distressed state. She was dressed to suggest that she was a young war widow, wearing a red, white and blue badge. As she set off on Thursday morning with her dispatch, she was spotted by some people who followed her to Dame Street and denounced her to some British soldiers.

Two British officers questioned her, and when her replies proved unsatisfactory, they insisted she go with them to Trinity College. She did not object, but decided to try and bluff her way out of the situation. At the gates of the college, she put the dispatch in her mouth and began to chew. One of the officers immediately asked her what she had in her mouth. Without any hesitation, she replied that it was a sweet, and taking a bag from her pocket, offered him a sweet, which was refused. Frank Robbins, a member of the ICA heard Caffrey's story on her return.

> The British officers then took her into a room and informed her they proposed to search her. She protested, tearfully expostulating that it was a poor tribute to the memory of her late husband who had 'given his life for the Empire'. They were not convinced and seeing this she demanded to be searched by one of her own sex. They were sorry, they retorted, to be unable to accommodate her with a woman searcher and proposed to do the job themselves. Without going into details Chris assured me they did a thorough job of work. Having found no incriminating evidence on her person they released her. When she gave me her account of this harrowing experience I could well understand her distressed state. But having related her story she was as collected as ever and awaited the next call of duty.[39]

The socialist historian, R. M. Fox, was given this account of this incident.

> After curfew she began her journey back to the College of Surgeons. At the Stephen's Green end of Grafton Street

bullets were flying. She nerved herself to run for the door, but to make it harder, the password had been changed and a stranger was on guard. He was suspicious and would not open. She banged and shouted frantically until another member of the garrison recognised her voice. When finally, the door was opened she stumbled in and fell unconscious to the floor.

She recovered to find Mallin bending over her. 'Did you deliver the dispatch?' he asked anxiously. 'No — I ate it!' she whispered.[40]

When she explained, Mallin told her she had done very well. Chris Caffrey later told Margaret Skinnider that she had been stripped by the soldiers before being searched.

During the week, some of the women who had shown leadership ability were promoted in rank. Madeleine ffrench-Mullen became a sergeant. The hard work and bravery of the women volunteers has been acknowledged by many of the men who worked beside them. One of many instances was later recounted by Commandant W. J. Brennan-Whitmore; this incident illustrates once again that Cumann na mBan members could be very determined about their right to make their own decisions. A temporary telephone had been hooked up between the GPO and the outpost next to the Imperial Hotel. It was used to relay messages about British troop movements. On Thursday, in the midst of heavy firing, the phone broke down.

> We had observed a movement of British troops towards the Quays which we could not bring under our fire effectively. It was essential that word should be promptly conveyed to the GPO. I called for a Volunteer to take the message, and despite the fact that it was tantamount to certain death to venture into O'Connell Street, everyone in the apartment stepped forward. [O'Connell Street was known as Sackville Street in 1916.]
>
> Amongst those Volunteers was a member of the Cumann na mBan — I regret very much that I do not remember her name — who insisted that she should take the message. On my demurring she stated that she had to go to the GPO for some extra bandages etc, and that she insisted on going for these, and that she might as well take the message. As I could not prevent her going on her own errand, which she

insisted on, and as the time was precious, I consented. We took down a portion of the barricade at one of the doors and helped her over it. She dashed across without a moment's hesitation. Our hearts were in our mouths as we watched, for it seemed that no human being could cross that broad thoroughfare without being riddled. But she negotiated it without mishap, and even returned in short time, laden with her Red Cross supplies.[41]

The unidentified Red Cross nurse who was present in this outpost, later recounted:

One one occasion in O'Connell Street, I heard a Volunteer captain call for volunteers to take a dispatch to Commandant James Connolly, under heavy machine gun fire. Every man and woman sprang forward, and he chose a young Dublin woman, a well known writer, whose relations hold big Crown appointments, and whom I had last seen dancing with an aide-de-camp at a famous Dublin ball. [It is possible that this was one of the Gifford sisters. However, Sydney Gifford, a journalist, was not in Dublin during the Rising.]

This girl had taken an extraordinarily daring part in the insurrection. She shook hands now with her commander and stepped cooly out amid a perfect cross-rain of bullets from Trinity College and from the Rotunda side of O'Connell Street. She reached the Post Office in safety and I saw Count Plunkett's son, who was the officer in charge and who has since been shot, come to the front door of the Post Office and wish her good luck as he shook hands with her before she made her reckless dash to take Connolly's dispatch back to her own headquarters.[42]

Margaret Skinnider Wounded

It was a firm rule among the insurgents that they should not engage the enemy when out of uniform. This was not just a principle — it was done to strengthen their case to be represented at the post-war international peace conference. Margaret Skinnider dressed in civilian clothes as she went about the city with her dispatches. On Wednesday, however, she was not busy, so Mallin agreed she could put on her uniform and join the snipers on the roof of the College of Surgeons. Later she was called down to deliver a dispatch and changed into a demure dress and hat. On her return, she changed back into uniform and went back to the roof.

It was on Wednesday that Skinnider's luck at dodging bullets came to an end. That evening, Skinnider and Joe Connolly approached Michael Mallin with a plan to bomb the Shelbourne Hotel and then escape by bicycle. Mallin agreed that the plan was a good one, but did not want a woman to undertake such a dangerous job.

> My answer to that argument was that we had the same right to risk our lives as the men; that in the constitution of the Irish Republic, women were on an equality with men. For the first time in history, indeed, a constitution had been written that incorporated the principle of equal suffrage.
>
> But the Commandant told me that there was another task to be accomplished before the hotel could be bombed. That was to cut off the retreat of a British force which had planted a machine gun on the roof of University Church. It was against our rules to use any church in our defence ... In order to cut off the retreat of those soldiers it would be necessary to burn some houses in Harcourt Street. I asked the commandant to let me help in this undertaking. He consented and gave me four men to help me fire one building ... It meant a great deal to me that he should trust me with this piece of work.[43]

As they reached the building to be fired, Skinnider was shot and had to be carried back wounded to the College of Surgeons. The men under her command for this operation included William Partridge and Fred Ryan, who was killed in the incident. In later years Nora Connolly referred to this incident as an example of the relationship which existed at the time between men and women in the Citizen Army. 'When they were going out to attack a nest of snipers she was in charge of the squad. William Partridge, a very famous man in the working-class movement, was there and he and other members of the squad accepted that she was in charge.'[44]

When Madeleine ffrench-Mullen cut away Skinnider's clothes, it was discovered that she had been hit three times, but Skinnider refused to go to hospital. She was not expected to live. Ffrench-Mullen went searching for a doctor, and after several had refused to come, she finally returned with a woman doctor named Dr Dillon.

On Thursday, during a lull in the shooting, Liam Ó Briain, who was positioned in a flat on St. Stephen's Green, received a message from Markievicz requesting that they find a nightdress for Margaret Skinnider. He found one and delivered it to the College of Surgeons, where he found a 'serious and grim air'[45] and a busy sick bay. Just before the surrender, Skinnider was taken to St. Vincent's Hospital, 'so that she would not fall wounded into the hands of the English'.[46] Markievicz managed to slip a copy of her will to Skinnider to take out for her.

Skinnider spent a total of seven weeks in hospital; amazingly, she was the only serious casualty among the women Volunteers. Skinnider occupied her time talking to the nurses about her work in Glasgow for women's suffrage and explaining about the Rising. After five weeks a detective arrested her, despite protests from the nurses. She was taken to the Bridewell and questioned about herself and the other women from Glasgow. Some time later, after the intervention of the hospital's head doctor, she was returned to the hospital, where she stayed for another two weeks. Skinnider was proud of the fact that she had received three mentions in dispatches to headquarters for her bravery during Easter Week.

5

A City on Fire

By Thursday the city was on fire and all medical personnel were under considerable pressure. James Ryan's medical team in the GPO consisted of three male members of the republican medical corps and twelve Cumann na mBan members. On Thursday they stayed inside the GPO watching the fires and singing with the Volunteers. The women in the kitchen were unaware that the front of the building was on fire.

At Jacob's, Máire Nic Shiubhlaigh climbed up on the roof and watched the GPO burning. Jacob's had been surrounded by hostile crowds for several days, but on Thursday, as they were cut off from the other insurgents, the mood of the crowd changed. Jacob's workers, sympathetic to the insurgents, had gathered around the factory and this saved it from attack by the British soldiers who would not fire on non-combatants.

Linda Kearns' field hospital was visited by a British officer, who insisted that she must limit her patients to members of the British military or close. She closed the hospital, sending her patients to the Mater and Temple Street hospitals. She spent the rest of the week working as a dispatch carrier and first-aid worker.

At about 10.30 a.m. on Thursday, Leslie Price rang the bell at the Pro-Cathedral; she had an urgent request for a priest to come to the GPO to attend a dying Volunteer. Father Flanagan answered the door. The priest was at first unwilling to go, because, he said, he believed it was possible to take the Volunteer to Jervis Street Hospital, where priests were on duty. After a somewhat risky trip by a circuitous route — Thomas Lane, Marlboro Street, Parnell Street, Moore Street, across Henry Street, into Randalls' hallway, upstairs, through gaps in walls of intervening houses — they reached the GPO, where, according to the priest, he received 'a hearty welcome from as gay and debonair an army as ever took up arms.'[1] The priest subsequently claimed that there was no dying Volunteer there in need of ministry; however he stayed with the GPO garrison until evacuation on Friday, going with the wounded to Jervis Street.

Leslie Price's memory of these events is strikingly different from Father Flanagan's. According to her, Tom Clarke called her and told her to go to Marlborough Street Church and bring back a priest. She was very frightened and presumed a Volunteer was dying. There was shooting going on in the street, 'But I knew I had to go on.'[2]

> I went on and I got to the steps of the presbytery. With the heel of my shoe I battered on the door. I was shivering there and after a while a priest came out to me ...
>
> He looked at me and he said, 'Do you realise that you're working in there with a group of communists, that you have James Connolly and all the socialists in there?' So I said, 'I have been sent for a priest.' 'I'm certain no man or woman in the General Post Office wants a priest,' he said. I knew that every one of us had gone to confession on Easter Saturday, but I thought, if a man is dying, it is a consolation to have a priest. So I said, 'If you don't want to come, I'm going back and I'm going back alone.'
>
> He considered for a bit and he talked still about the socialists and the communists and what not and he said, 'You're a very foolish child. You should be at home with your parents!'[3]

The priests of the Pro-Cathedral were called upon again for assistance later in the week. It was decided to evacuate the North Earl Street outpost. The women of the garrison 'rejected with scorn'[4] the suggestion that they should leave in the interests of their personal safety. The commandant of the Volunteers,

W.J. Brennan-Whitmore, was in a quandary. The men refused to take the women along because they believed it was too dangerous; on the other hand they were not inclined to 'leave them to their own devices in the dark of night'.[5]

> Learning that there was a priest's house attached to the Pro-Cathedral I at once proceeded to it and knocked upon the door. It was opened almost at once, and a priest appearing, asked me if I wanted sanctuary. I replied that I did, for some ladies. After a good deal of persuasion, and not a little shoving, we got the ladies inside and saw the door closed behind them.[6]

The women, who had to be lifted bodily into the house, were left locked inside. The men were later trapped nearby and arrested the next day.

One woman who did leave, but on a courier mission, was Annie Higgins. She was a talented musician and composer, who invented a new method of teaching harmony, which she used in her work as a music teacher. At the time of the Rising she was on holiday from her teaching post in Carrickmacross. She spent Tuesday and Wednesday morning cooking for the Volunteers at the Hibernian Bank, until they evacuated to the GPO at about midday.

On Thursday, she was sent north, although her account does not reveal exactly what item(s) she had to deliver.

> I left the city about 1 p.m., and used my return ticket to Carrick as a passport, getting safely past the military cordons by that means. I borrowed a bicycle from a girl who lives just outside the city, and cycled to Swords. Unfortunately my ankles had swollen dreadfully, and I was not able to go any further than night, but some friends put me up for the night and on the next morning I set out again.
>
> I cycled to Drogheda and got a train there to Carrickmacross and delivered my –. The first thing I heard when I got to Carrick was that the police had sent down to a hotel to see if I was there. I did not go to the hotel until about 11 o'clock that night, and the next morning I walked boldly up the Main Street, past the police barracks to the Convent, with my bicycle — and out the other gate.
>
> I set out for Ballinagh, the police believing I was safe in the Convent! At Kingscourt, my bicycle broke down and I

obtained a motor. I did Bailieboro', Kilnaleck, Ballinagh
and Cavan that day, and as you know, when I got back to
Kingscourt was arrested.[7]

When arrested and taken to Armagh Jail, her ankles were
badly swollen and she was on the point of collapse. Higgins
lost her job as a result of her arrest.

Enniscorthy Joins the Rising

As the situation in Dublin became increasingly desperate,
decisive action was finally being taken in Enniscorthy, one of
the few areas outside of Dublin to fight. Here, the republicans'
weapons consisted of homemade pikes, a few carbines, shotguns
and Howth rifles, some revolvers and grenades. On Thursday
morning they marched to the Athenaeum and took it over. The
Volunteers were fully supported by the local Cumann na mBan
under the command of Mary White. Seumas Ó Dubhghaill, a
leader of the Volunteers, was to comment: 'I believe that not a
single member of this organisation failed us — their patriotism
was magnificent.'[8]

The women set up cooking and first aid operations in the
skating rink next to the Athenaeum. Working with them were
schoolteacher Eileen O'Hegarty and Una Brennan from
Wexford. The Tricolour was hoisted above the Athenaeum by
Una Brennan (secretary of Enniscorthy Cumann na mBan),
Marion Stokes and Gretta Comerford. Kate Browr of Wexford
was among those arrested.

Ashbourne Fights

On Easter Sunday, there was a full mobilisation of the
Volunteers in Ashbourne, County Dublin, but then the Sunday
paper containing the countermand arrived. The men dispersed,
but at 7 a.m. Monday, Joseph Lawless was awakened by his
aunt, Miss Adrian, who had cycled from Dublin with Pearse's
message: "Strike at one o'clock today". The Ashbourne column,
which fought under Thomas Ashe, consisted of about forty-
five men. Early in the week they were involved in a number of
skirmishes with the RIC, and on Tuesday, they received a

request for twenty men to be sent to Dublin and the rest used to create a diversion. On Friday they attacked the barracks at Ashbourne, and inflicted heavy casualties on the numerically superioir RIC. Miss Adrian cycled back and forth from the GPO throughout the week, carrying messages and orders for the Ashbourne Volunteers.

Women Quit Coalisland

One day Nora Connolly was in a hotel in Coalisland when a man rushed in, calling for the 'first aiders'. A man had shot himself in the thumb. The wound was not serious and Nora bandaged it without trouble while a group of men looked on impressed. A man clapped her on the shoulder and said, 'You're the one for us!' Nora, frustrated by her days of inactivity replied, 'Fine, but how do you know but that I want to make holes, not plug them.'[9]

There were no newspapers, but rumours reached them in abundance.

> The Germans had landed in Donegal — the Dublin Brigade had been wiped out — Dublin had been cleared of all English troops — the West was 'up' — the fight was over. We did not know what to believe so refused to believe anything.[10]

Thursday evening Kathleen's brother arrived in Coalisland with orders for the Belfast Cumann na mBan members to return to Belfast. Nora Connolly refused to go. She said she would locate her sister and they would go to Dublin. The other women left Tyrone on Friday morning with an escort to Belfast, leaving all their precious equipment in the country.

Éilis Ní Chorra was a typist in the Belfast public library, and on her return from Tyrone was called before the library authorities and asked if she had been fighting in Dublin. She retorted that she would have been if she had had the chance and was dismissed for being absent without leave. After the Rising, she, like many others, threw herself into organising the relief fund for the families of the dead and imprisoned.

On Friday, Nora and Ina Connolly set off from Coalisland by train and got as far as Dundalk. Then they had to get off, as only the military were being allowed on the trains. They started to walk.

> We spent the night in a field, shaking with the cold. We got near Balbriggan, exhausted and footsore. We went into a ploughed field, took off our shoes and stockings and plunged our poor feet into the rich, cool, brown earth and I think we dozed off because we were awakened by the thunder of gunfire. Off we went.[11]

Dirty and exhausted, they reached the Ryans' house on Clonliffe Road on Saturday 29 April. The Ryans broke the news that James Connolly was dying. The sisters left immediately to walk across Dublin to be with their mother.

> It was terrible! All the buildings in ruins. We passed Cathedral Lane. There were dead horses lying there and that horrible smell of burning everywhere. The GPO was in absolute ruins but the flag was still flying.[12]

Retreat

By Friday, the women in the GPO garrison included 31 members of Cumann na mBan, two members of the Citizen Army and one member of Clann na nGaedheal. The male leaders decided that it was time for some of the women to leave. The women did not want to go and held a discussion among themselves, but most decided to go because they felt that in the worsening situation they might be an encumbrance to the men. Some women, however, were not prepared to leave, but Pearse insisted. Twelve women were asked to stay. At about noon, Pearse called together those who were going and shook each woman's hand. They deserved, he said, a foremost place in the history of the nation. A group of about 20 left in the early afternoon; they were to take some of the wounded to Jervis Street hospital and, while they waited to leave, they collected messages from the men to take to their families.

Because of its central location, Jervis Street hospital took in a large proportion of the Rising's casualties. Many of the staff went out of their way to assist the rebels. A hole in the wall of the hospital, which allowed direct access from the GPO through the Henry Street houses, was hidden by wardrobes and screens; wounded rebels arriving at the hospital were quickly hidden. When the British military came to search the hospital, they found everything apparently operating routinely. Dr. J. C. O'Carroll, a student resident in the hospital at the time, was instructed by the Reverend Mother to escort them and to use his 'best tony accent'[13] and charm. O'Carroll described how insurgents able to walk were disguised as wardsmaids: 'Everything was under control; sisters and nurses going about their duties and wardsmaids pushing polishers up and down the corridors. Had the officers looked at the big feet of some of the wardsmaids they wouldn't have had their raid for nothing.'[14] On one such occasion, Miss Kelly, superintendent of the nurses, accompanied O'Carroll and the British officers. When they entered the nun's ward, O'Carroll was startled to see the drammatically increased number of bed-ridden nuns, their heads covered in white wimples. However, 'Matron's sharp eyes had a quelling look, though her smile was sweet and innocent and her voice steady and determined.'[15]

When wounded insurgents arrived at the hospital all their clothing and other incriminating possessions, such as sheets of stamps taken from the GPO, were taken away and burned by the nurses.

> They burned everything: boots, hats, uniforms. You would think there was a rebellion every day in the week to look at them. They needed no-one to tell them what to do. One young Nurse cut off her long plaits and pinned them to an unconscious boy's head. Her only worry was to get them off again before he recovered consciousness. Another young man awoke to consciousness after an operation for removal of bullets to find a bonny baby in his arms.[16]

Louise Gavan Duffy told how on the way they met a British officer and a group of soldiers who accompanied them to the hospital. The nuns at the hospital took the wounded and quickly 'lost' them among the patients. The British officer escorted the healthy men from the hospital. (The women were convinced that the men were to be shot, but on Sunday they learned that the men had been released.) The nuns suggested that the women spend the night at the hospital because it was very dangerous outside; they slept on the floor of a waiting room.

Leslie Price remembered these events slightly differently.

> ... we took the wounded up to Jervis Street hospital and then we realised we'd only be in the way there. So, at the corner of Capel Street looking down Mary Street there was a barricade of British soldiers and we were called there by the officer. The officer-in-charge, I suppose 'twas an NCO, said to take us up to Broadstone, that we were prisoners. So we were marched off up there and on the way, you see, Louise Gavan Duffy had whispered to some of the others and 'twas passed down to some of us who knew the nuns in Eccles Street, that when we'd be brought before the military for questioning at Broadstone that we would say we were students from the school, that we had been out for a walk down O'Connell Street and we were ordered to go into the General Post Office. So we were brought in one by one and some of us spun this story, and it was taken, accepted, and then we were told, 'Well, you can go back to the school.' So I needn't tell you we did march back to Eccles Street in case anyone was behind us. When we got in there the nuns gave us tea and we were able to go home.[17]

On Saturday morning, they heard that the Volunteers had surrendered. The women were unsure what to do so they split up. Louise Gavan Duffy headed to her Dublin home, arriving without coat or hat and 'very tired and dirty'.[18] On the way she met two college students she knew. 'When they saw me they put around the rumour that I had been wounded, but it was nothing as heroic as that. I was simply limping from having spent the whole week without being able to take my shoes off.'[19]

According to Leslie Price:

> The person who was in charge of the commissariat, the woman who was magnificent, was Louise Gavan Duffy. She was the greatest inspiration any woman or girl could have. She never got off her feet. I'd say she hardly got one hour's sleep the whole week and the last that I saw of her, her feet were very swollen.[20]

Later on Saturday, Louise Gavan Duffy, May Murray and Peggy Downey went to Jacob's factory and told John McBride and Thomas MacDonagh what was happening elsewhere.

MacDonagh asked them not to tell the others in his garrison how badly Connolly was hurt and told them to come back on Monday if the fight was still on.

Only three women had remained in the GPO after the evacuation: Winifred Carney, Julia Grenan and Elizabeth O'Farrell. On Friday, Pearse had approached Winifred Carney and asked if she would insist on remaining. She told him that she had no intention of leaving. By evening, it was impossible to stay in the GPO any longer.

The building was entirely in flames and the British kept up a continuous heavy fire. The remaining garrison left by the side entrance into Henry Street. There was a barricade in Moore Lane, and the military were firing over it. Elizabeth O'Farrell was one of the last to leave: 'bullets [were] raining from all quarters as we rushed to Moore Lane. As I passed the barricade I tripped and fell ...'[21] Sean McGarry rushed out and lifted her to safety.

Seventeen men were wounded and four men, including The O'Rahilly, were killed during this evacuation. Linda Kearns was working as a stretcher bearer in Moore Street when The O'Rahilly was shot. By the time she could reach him, he was dead.

> I was in Moore Street on the afternoon when The O'Rahilly was killed. One of the stretcher-bearers was with me, and we saw him lying in the path, and went over to him, and found he was dead. But life must have only just left him, for he was quite warm.[22]

The house in Moore Street where the remnants of the GPO garrison had taken shelter was full of wounded men — those who had been hurt in the evacuation and others who had been transferred on stretchers from the GPO, including James Connolly and a badly injured British soldier. Elizabeth O'Farrell, Winifred Carney and Julia Grenan were kept busy all night helping to nurse them. Some of the Volunteers gave Winifred Carney small mementoes and messages for their families. Joseph Plunkett gave her a filigree bangle and a ring to pass on to his fiancée, Grace Gifford.

6
Saturday — the Surrender

Number 16 Moore Street became the headquarters for the Provisional Council of the Republic. The able-bodied men of the GPO garrison had spent the night breaking holes in the walls of the adjoining houses and the wounded, including James Connolly, were carried through to this, the end house of the row. Gathered for a council of war around Connolly's bed were Padraic and Willie Pearse, Joseph Plunkett, Thomas Clarke and Seán MacDiarmada.

More and more of the city was being destroyed and civilians were being brutalised and killed by the British forces. This widespread victimisation of non-combatants was the decisive factor in the decision to surrender. Seán MacDiarmada came to Elizabeth O'Farrell and asked her to make a white flag. Tom Clarke was standing by the window. He broke down and Winifred Carney went to him, only to burst into tears herself. They held each other for a few moments. O'Farrell recalled:

> I left the house ... with a verbal message from Commandant Pearse to the Commander of the British forces, to the effect that he wished to treat with them. I waved the small white flag which I carried and the military ceased firing.[1]

Julia Grenan wept, thinking her dearest friend was walking to certain death. James Connolly called her over to his bedside and said to her: 'Don't be crying for your friend. They won't shoot her. They may blindfold her and bring her across their lines to wherever their Commandant is, so she may be away for some time. But they won't shoot her.'[2] The atmosphere in the house was very sad. Pearse went round each of the men and women, saying goodbye. Winifred Carney knelt beside Connolly's bed, weeping, and asking, 'Was there no other way?' Connolly said that he could not bear to see his brave boys burned to death and that there was no other way.[3]

The main reason for the decision to surrender, however, was the burning of the city and the wholesale slaughter of non-combatants, which had not been anticipated by the republican leadership. A member of Columcille branch of Cumann na mBan was to write later:

> Monday afternoon, May 1, some of us girls went through North King Street and the deadhouses in the Richmond Union hospitals. It was a gruesome sight to see the dead piled on top of each other in the morgues where there were not enough marble slabs on which to place the bodies. Some lay in their clothes just as they had fallen, and so close to each other that one had to go sideways to pass through. It was pitiful to see the women going around from one house of death to another and to the hospitals looking for husbands, fathers or brothers, not knowing where they were or where to look for them. [...]
>
> We proceeded on our way through North King Street, and in one part near the military headquarters the scene was appalling. In the first house we entered a father and his only child lay dead in their clothes, just as they had fallen, and the poor wife was sitting there dazed and oblivious to what was going on around her, gazing silently at her husband and child, all she had in this world.
>
> We went into another house and saw a man lying there dead, with a cloth across his throat. We inquired what had happened and were told he had been shot in the presence of his wife and children and then a soldier had bayoneted him. ... Almost every house in this portion of North King Street held either a corpse or an injured person. [...]
>
> Everyone spoke of the brutal conduct of the military in North King Street, even the Loyalists had to admit that their conduct was disgraceful. ...dead bodies of young girls, matrons and elderly women, lying in twos and threes in the halls, stairways and cellars, bore mute and terrible testimony

to the horrible and unspeakable outrages of the cowardly
ruffians who wear the livery of Britain.[4]

When Elizabeth O'Farrell reached the British lines at the
corner of Moore Street and Parnell Street, the commanding
officer came out to speak to her.

> I said: 'Commandant of the Irish Republican Army wishes
> to treat with the Commandant of the British Forces in
> Ireland.'
> Officer: 'Irish Republican Army — the Sinn Feiners you
> mean.'
> I replied: 'The Irish Republican Army they call themselves
> and I think that a very good name too.'
> Officer: 'Will Pearse be able to be moved on a stretcher?'
> I said: 'Pearse doesn't need a stretcher.'
> Officer: 'Pearse does need a stretcher, madam.'
> I again answered: 'Commandant Pearse doesn't need a
> stretcher.'
> To another officer: 'Take that Red Cross off her and bring
> her over there and search her — she is a spy.'
> The officer, as ordered, proceeded to cut the Red Cross
> off my arm, also off the front of my apron, and then took me
> over to the hall of the National Bank on the corner of Parnell
> Street and Cavendish Row, where he searched me and found
> two pairs of scissors (one of which he afterwards returned
> to me), some sweets, bread, and cakes etc. Being satisfied
> that I wasn't dangerous he then took me (of all places in the
> world) to Tom Clarke's shop as a prisoner — all this
> procedure occupied about three-quarters of an hour.[5]

The British Brigadier-General Lowe arrived and from this
point she was treated courteously. He sent her back to Moore
Street with a message for Pearse that he would accept only an
unconditional surrender. She was told that unless she returned
within half an hour with Pearse and Connolly, hostilities would
be resumed. On her way back, she passed the body of The
O'Rahilly, still lying in Moore Street where he had died the
day before.

Among the rank and file in 16 Moore Street there was still
considerable discontent about the decision to surrender. Tom
Clarke talked about his lifelong commitment to the struggle
and said that he was satisfied, and that they should they be also.

About 3.30 p.m., Pearse came out and walked to the corner of Moore Street and Parnell Street, where he surrendered his sword to Lowe. (In the well-known photograph of Pearse surrendering to General Lowe, Pearse appears to be wearing a long greatcoat. In fact, Elizabeth O'Farrell is standing next to him and it is her long skirt that shows in the photograph.) Pearse shook hands with Elizabeth O'Farrell and she agreed to stay with the British and take the surrender order to the rest of the garrisons, with the promise that she would then be set free.

The rest of the GPO garrison filed out of the house behind Willie Pearse, who carried the white flag. Winifred Carney and Julia Grenan were near the back of the line. Grenan recalled:

> We came out of the house ... and on the edge of the path at Henry Place, there was a Volunteer and the Volunteer had his hands outstretched and when I saw him like that, I thought of the poor old croppy stretched out on the mountain-side. God help him, he was turned towards the wall. This poor fellow, he certainly looked very noble he did, very noble looking.
>
> So, we went up O'Connell Street then and the British soldiers were at the corner of Henry Street and they swinging their revolvers cursing us into the ground and out of it. However we went up and we were put sitting and lying on the grass plot.[6]

On Friday night, Commandant Daly had decided to transfer his headquarters from the Father Mathew Hall to the Four Courts. By this time the hall was full of wounded and could not be defended. By Saturday morning, the British forces were closing in and the sound of rifle fire was deafening. Volunteers in the nearby outposts had all retreated to the Four Courts.

By about 4 p.m. on Saturday, the situation inside the hall was very tense. Fighting in the area had been heavy all night and major fires raged nearby. The hall held many wounded, including some very bad cases. The military had reached North King Street and were firing on the barricade at the hall. Those inside expected the building would be shelled at any time. The priests present sent two messengers to the British explaining that the hall was in use as a hospital and requesting that serious cases be allowed to transfer to an outside hospital. The reply came back that none of the amenities of war would be granted, but that they would be treated as outlaws and rebels. Two of the priests then set out themselves to meet the military and were informed that a truce had been arranged. The republicans fighting in the area were sceptical, but agreed to stop fighting until Pearse could be contacted.

The priests returned to Father Mathew Hall and told the nursing staff they could go home. According to Father Aloysius, some of the staff from Richmond Hospital were in the hall and arranged for the transfer of patients. The hall was cleared quickly. The less seriously wounded escaped to safe houses and the women carried the rest to hospital on stretchers. Éilis Ní Rian helped bring in the last stretcher. One of the doctors put a hand on her shoulder. She froze, imagining he was going to have her arrested, but he only asked if she had had any sleep during the week and said that the women had done 'trojan work' with the wounded.[7] The hospital was later raided, but no one was arrested.

Éilis returned to Father Mathew Hall at about 11 p.m. It was now virtually empty; only two priests, the Elliot sisters and Kathleen Kenny remained. Father Augustine suggested that they stay in the church until morning. He organised a small room next to the high altar with bedding from the hospital and an electric fire. They were told to leave in the morning when the Angelus bells rang, before the church doors opened, then attend Mass and mingle with the congregation when leaving.

The women could not sleep; they feared for their comrades and the noise outside was deafening. In the morning the priest brought them tea and bread and butter. This was very welcome, because the women had 'not tasted food for some time.'[8] At Mass they saw a number of male Volunteers, who like them melted into the congregation. Two of the women returned to the Father Mathew Hall, cooked breakfast for themselves and the men who remained there and burned whatever papers, dispatches and other incriminating material they found there. Éilis Ní Rian and her companions were not able to go directly home:

> We wended our way for home back through the narrow
> streets. Every street corner was now lined with armed British
> Tommies and after zig-zagging from one street to another
> to avoid the soldiers, we reached North Frederick Street in
> the evening.[9]

They had not eaten all day, excepting the early morning bread
and tea. At the Gaelic League office they met two members of
the Keating branch who escorted them to the restaurant run by
the Misses Molloy where they had tea. From there they made
their way to Fleming's Hotel in Gardiner Place where they met
Katy McGuinness and Sorcha McMahon. They washed and
ate and talked of the surrender and the confusing events. The
city was now under martial law, so they left soon to reach home
before the curfew.

After taking the order to surrender to the republican forces in
Moore Street, Elizabeth O'Farrell started towards the Four
Courts. She was stopped along the way by several British
officers. Further on, she met Father Columbus, who offered to
accompany her. At the Four Courts the Volunteers were strongly
entrenched. O'Farrell met the commandant of the garrison,
Edward Daly and gave him the order to surrender, which he
accepted reluctantly.

When she left the Four Courts, Elizabeth O'Farrell made her
way back up O'Connell Street and reported to the British
Lieutenant Colonel Owens, who took her to the National Bank.
She spent the night in a bedroom at the back of the house, with
a British officer sitting on a chair outside her door. She woke
about 6 a.m. From the window she could see Julia Grenan and
Winifred Carney lying on the grass in front of the Rotunda.
Soldiers had cut the red crosses from their uniforms and they
had spent the night with 300-400 other prisoners without food
or shelter. Winifred Carney described the scene:

> Sean MacDiarmada is sitting beside me. Close by is Brian
> O'Higgins. Sean gives me some compressed food lozenges.
> They tasted awful. Meanwhile the soldiers keep up a constant
> cross-talk, using filthy expressions ... I feel my blood boil,
> many of the boys are so young and have been to Communion
> before the Rising. I whispered to Sean what I would do if I

had my revolver and he puts his arm around me, afraid I
may attempt something foolish ... I remember a boy whom
an officer pushed with his foot ... I told the boy to keep
closer to me. He never murmured but the cold touch of his
body like ice penetrated through me.[10]

They were surrounded by police and military and machine
guns were trained on them from the roofs above. They were
ordered to lie down and told that if they attempted to rise above
their knees they would be shot.

The prisoners were herded together in the Rotunda gardens,
and acting on express order of their officers, the British
troops set upon them with clubbed rifles and smashed right
and left among them, beating them in a most savage
manner.[11]

James Connolly gave his coat to Winifred Carney. She laid it
with her own on the ground for Joseph Plunkett and Seán
MacDiarmada, who were suffering from the cold. The next
day the prisoners were taken to Richmond Barracks and then to
Kilmainham Jail.

Elizabeth O'Farrell was driven to Grafton Street by the British
officer, Major Wheeler, and from there walked to the College
of Surgeons carrying a white flag and typed copies of the
surrender order. Bullets continued to whizz around the Green.
She gave the order first to Markievicz, who woke Mallin, and
the members of the garrison were called together in the College
of Surgeons to hear him read it aloud.

The men and women in the College of Surgeons were
distraught at the news of the surrender. They had determined to
hold out till the end and did not understand why the order was
made. It was only because the order was signed by James
Connolly himself that it was accepted. Markievicz went round
the republicans repeating over and over: 'I trust James Connolly,
I trust James Connolly.'[12] Mallin had to repeat this painful duty
three times, as new groups of republicans came in from the
outposts.

In the College of Surgeons garrison there were 110
republicans at the surrender. Douglas Hyde wrote in his diary
for the day:

> Met Father Sherwin in the street ... he brought me the important intelligence that the men in the College of Surgeons had at last this afternoon hung out the white flag and surrendered. These men had dominated the whole of Stephen's Green since Monday and until they surrendered at 2 o'clock today no soldier dared show his face inside the Green though they themselves passed in and out of it freely. He said that the positions around Stephen's Green had been chosen with much strategic ability. I asked him how many had been taken prisoner and he said he saw them come out and that there were about 100 and a good many of them were women who shot as well as the men. I suppose these were the Countess Markievicz's girls.[13]

That the garrison had held out against fearsome odds even the pro-British *Irish Times* acknowledged.

> Day after day, and night after night, the sniping continued until the rebels had been severely punished. Towards the end of the week the Green was evacuated but the firing continued from the College of Surgeons, and from other houses where Sinn Feiners were concealed. The Countess Markievicz was in command of the rebels here.
>
> The Royal College of Surgeons in St. Stephen's Green was one of the last 'forts' to capitulate. After a week's occupation the surrender took place at two o'clock in the afternoon of Sunday 30th ult. Major John Wheeler, son of the late Surgeon Wheeler, accompanied by a force of military, attendant at that hour and was received by the rebel leader, the Countess Markievicz. She was still wearing top boots, breeches, service tunic and a hat with feathers. In the presence of the military she first shook hands with her 'soldiers' and then produced her revolver; passionately kissing the weapon, she handed it to Major Wheeler, together with a quantity of ammunition, which on examination was found to include military and also round (expanding) bullets.[14]

The *Irish Times* got its information from the British military, and it was Major Wheeler's report that first contained the story of Markievicz kissing her revolver. This story has since been used as an example of Markievicz's supposedly bloodthirsty and eccentric nature, even though it was denied at the time. On 3 May, the artist Sarah Purser, who was a family friend of the Gore-Booths, wrote in her diary:

> I am thankful that none of the people I am really acquainted
> with even or came much in contact with are among those
> who have risen except Con Markievicz ... I did not think she
> would let herself be taken but am glad at least to hear the
> histrionics of her kissing her revolver etc., denied.[15]

First-aid worker Nora Foley recorded: 'We were marched
out into York Street, men first, women following. I carried the
Red Cross flag, as some extraordinary stories were afloat to
account for the presence of women amongst the garrisons.'[16]
As they passed the gates of Richmond Barracks, a soldier on a
bicycle snatched the flag out of her hand. Inside the barracks,
a guard was placed on the women's cell — to protect them
from the soldiers.

After delivering the surrender order to the College of
Surgeons, Elizabeth O'Farrell returned to Captain Wheeler's
car. He decided to take her next to Boland's Mills, but the way
was blocked by barricades. At Butts Bridge, he told O'Farrell
that he could not take her any further.

> So I started through the firing line from Butts Bridge to
> Boland's. I did not know whether the Volunteers were still
> in Boland's or not, so I had to go up to Westland Row to the
> military to ask them to locate the Volunteers for me. This
> was a very difficult job and I had to take my life in my hands
> several times. When I came to Westland Row the military
> were lined across the top, and they were screaming at me to
> go back, but I kept waving my white flag and the paper.[17]

She made her way through the dangerous streets, first to the
gasworks, then the old distillery and on to the bakery. She got
no reply from the Volunteers. Then, near the railway bridge,
she saw some Volunteers who knew her and told her de Valera
was at the Grand Canal Street Dispensary.

> I went off to the Dispensary, back again towards town, and
> crossing Grand Canal Street Bridge, the firing was terrific.
> At this point a man crossing the bridge about half a yard
> behind me was shot. I called to some people in houses down
> the street, and they ran up and carried him into Sir Patrick
> Dun's Hospital.[18]

At the dispensary some barricades had to be removed and
she was lifted in through the window. De Valera came in and at

first thought her message was a hoax. But some Volunteers who knew her assured him she was to be trusted. He then said that he could not take any order except from his immediate commanding officer, MacDonagh. 'So after my trouble in finding him I had to go off again.'[19]

She was taken to Jacob's to find MacDonagh. When she got there she was blindfolded and walked for about five minutes, then was allowed to see MacDonagh and explained the situation. At first MacDonagh refused to accept an order from Pearse given in the circumstances of him being held a prisoner. He ordered the Tricolour to be raised over Jacob's to show that the garrison had not surrendered.

MacDonagh believed that they had ample supplies to hold their position for some weeks and was convinced that if the republican forces could hold out for a week or two their case would be certain to go before the international peace conference. But after going to Marrowbone Lane to discuss with Eamonn Ceannt, he called in first the Volunteer officers, then Máire nic Shiubhlaigh, who was the ranking officer of Cumann na mBan in the garrison.

O'Farrell recalled his words to the men: 'Boys, it is not my wish to surrender, but after consultation with Cmdt Ceannt and other officers, we think it is the best thing to do — if we do not surrender now they will show no mercy to the leaders who are already prisoners.'[20]

Some of the men asked O'Farrell to take the money they carried to their families. She then went out into the street and waited. Nic Shiubhlaigh recalled that MacDonagh was very business-like, but that his voice betrayed disillusion. 'He said, "I want you to thank all the girls for what they have done. Tell them I am issuing an order they are all to go home. I'll see that you are all safely conducted out of the building." I started to protest, but he turned away.'[21] MacDonagh wanted the women out of the building before he surrendered.

By the time Máire nic Shiubhlaigh returned to the bakeroom, the news had spread. Everyone was greatly upset and some of the men started breaking their rifles. Then a member of Cumann na mBan suggested that the proper way to surrender was to march out as soldiers with their weapons and surrender their arms formally. The garrison agreed to do this. The order was for all the men in civilian dress to leave and those in uniform to stay. All the men refused to leave. Máire nic Shiubhlaigh gave her order to the women, but they too were reluctant to leave. Seventeen-year-old Sara Kealy suggested that it might be useful if the women stayed to write letters for the men and carry messages to their relatives. She said she would stay. Nic Shiubhlaigh could not bring herself to press the matter.

On Sunday morning Louise Gavan Duffy called on Máire (Min) Ryan and together they set out to find out what was happening around the city. They arrived at St. Stephen's Green as some of the garrison were being brought out.

> They were a pitiful sight, the poor lads, after a week — and only twenty or thirty of them there, dirty, scruffy but in good spirit. There were a crowd of onlookers staring at them, not speaking a word as if they either resented the Volunteers or were afraid of the soldiers. Just as the prisoners were being taken away, however, one of the crowd roared out encouragement to the lads and the rest of the crowd joined in. At that moment my heart filled with pride for the people of Dublin, and I'm sure it was a source of great heart for the lads, that shout.[22]

The two women arrived at Jacob's shortly after the order to surrender was given there. MacDonagh came in then and once more asked the women to leave. He was told they wanted to stay. John McBride intervened to say it would be better if they left. The women finally agreed because they did not wish their presence to be a further worry and upset for the men. When they left the building they were escorted across the street by a British officer. Louise Gavan Duffy and Min Ryan urged Máire Nic Shiubhlaigh to go home with them.

At about 6 p.m. while Elizabeth O'Farrell was waiting outside Jacob's, Eamonn Ceannt came down Ross Road and surrendered with the Volunteers and Cumann na mBan members under his command. They were disarmed, by the British. Major Wheeler was deciding whether to return to Boland's Mills when he received word to take O'Farrell to Dublin Castle. De Valera had in the meantime surrendered.

The Marrowbone Distillery was well fortified and well provisioned when the surrender order reached the distillery. Con Colbert refused to believe it until Eamonn Ceannt came to confirm it personally. Here the uniformed forces of Cumann na mBan marched out in rows of four along with the men. There were 22 women at the surrender under the leadership of Miss MacNamara; some of them carried arms. They could have evaded arrest, but chose formal surrender instead. Nell Gifford explained the thinking of many of the women: 'The Republic promised us equality without sex distinction, so we were all adjudged soldiers, women and men, whether we worked as dispatch carriers or red cross units.'[23] The republicans marched out singing 'The Soldier's Song'. After the surrender they were attacked by an ill-disposed crowd of soldiers' wives and had to be defended by British soldiers with fixed bayonets. The prisoners were taken to Kilmainham jail.

Brighid Lyons had spent most of the week in a small outpost of the Four Courts garrison, making tea and sandwiches and tending to the injured. Brighid was a member of Cumann na mBan in Longford, where her family were small farmers. Her father had been in prison for his involvement in the Fenian movement and she was a niece of Joe and Katy McGuinness, both leading republicans who were also attached to the Four Courts garrison. On the Tuesday after Easter, one of her uncles in Longford had suggested they travel to Dublin to find out what was happening. She had agreed immediately and had likewise taken the first opportunity to lend a hand once there.

On Saturday, a rumour went round of surrender and a silence 'louder than all the noise'[24] descended on the city. Some of the men gave Brighid messages for their families; one gave her his gun, which she put in the pocket of her skirt. She recalled many years later,

> They had all bought their own guns, you see, and there were
> no supplies from Libya or Russia or anywhere else, and
> they'd do anything rather than give them up. So then towards
> evening we did hear that we had surrendered. It was a terrible

shattering, chaotic moment. They cried and they wept and they protested and they did their best to destroy their guns. I could see them hacking away at them. But there was no escape for them then.[25]

Later, some poor people from the area came in looking for food. Brighid gave away the bread and ham that she had in her charge and decided to make her way back to the Four Courts. Joe McGuinness asked her to take a message back to Katy, but Commandant Daly at once told her not to leave, as the city was under martial law. A British officer, Lieutenant Lindsay, was with him; he had given his word of honour that the women would be allowed to go home in the morning. 'After that we were sent upstairs and some of the Church Street priests came in and lambasted us with abuse all night for doing what we did.'[26]

The next morning they were told they would not be going home, but were being taken to Richmond Barracks. The women and some men were put on the back of a lorry and driven through the city. Later they were moved to Kilmainham. At Kilmainham jail a large and antagonistic crowd of 'Separation' women had gathered outside the gates.

> Now we never had the British to protect us before, but luckily the soldiers guarded us very heavily, because when the gates were opened and we were marched out there were such shrieks of hatred. Never did I see such savage women ... A lot of it seemed to be directed against the Countess' breeches and puttees.[27]

When Elizabeth O'Farrell woke on Monday morning, she found that her clothes had been taken away in the night, along with the money she had been given by Volunteers. She was given back her clothes. She protested about the confiscation of the money and said that she had been assured by Brigardier-General Lowe she would not be made a prisoner. The officer in charge replied,

> 'Oh, don't worry, you won't be lonely, as your friends, Dr. Lynn and Miss Molony, and all the rest, will be here in a few minutes — they are only taking exercise.' I discovered the place was Ship Street Barracks. In the room was a couple

of tables and a plank affair, something like a bed on the floor. After some time Dr Lynn, Miss Molony and nine others came in, and were quite surprised to see me — those eleven women had been lodged in this small room from the previous Tuesday. We then had dinner, consisting of bully-beef, biscuits and water provided by the military, and to this fare I contributed a barnbrack, an apple and a few sweets, which I had since I left the GPO on Friday night.[28]

Elizabeth O'Farrell made a number of futile protests against her imprisonment. The women were brought downstairs and told they were going to Kilmainham. Just then she saw the priest who had walked with her to the Four Courts and he promised to see General Lowe immediately. The women were marched to Kilmainham and put in the same cell. O'Farrell was the first to be called out.

I was called out first and brought into another cell, where I was stripped of my clothing and searched by two female warders. My clothes were also searched, and no dangerous weapons being concealed on me, I put on my coat and boots, carried all my other clothes under my arms, and was conducted to another cell, and locked in to dress at my leisure. After about a quarter of an hour the cell door was opened and Miss Molony, Miss ffrench-Mullen and another girl were put in and the door locked again. While we were chatting, the door was again opened and four tins slid in about the floor — this was our supper. It was awful stuff, neither soup nor stirabout, and while I was sampling it a terrible commotion was being raised outside the door, keys were rattled, the door pushed in, and I was called for, in terrible haste. I went outside to behold, in an apologetic attitude, the officer who had searched my clothes, taken away my money, and put me into the Ship Street Barracks that morning. He begged my pardon for the mistake.[29]

When she got downstairs she found Major Wheeler waiting, full of apologies. He took her to Dublin Castle, where she met Brigardier-General Lowe, who was upset that O'Farrell had been questioning his honour. She protested again about having been stripped and searched. The general insisted it had all been a mistake and ordered that the confiscated money be returned.

Members of Cumann na mBan, Irish Citizen Army and Clann na nGaedheal who took part in the Rising at the GPO, Jacob's, Marrowbone Lane, South Dublin Union and College of Surgeons garrisons. The photograph was taken in the garden of Mr & Mrs Ely O'Carroll, Peter's Place, Dublin, summer 1916 at a meeting of the National Aid Association.

The picture includes: A. Tobin, Aoife Taafe, Marcella Cosgrove, Mrs Murphy, Miss Foley, Martha Kelly, Máire Nic Shiúbhlaigh, Lily O'Brennan, Elizabeth O'Farrell, Nora Daly, May Murray, M. Kelly, Bridget Brady, Jenny Shanahan, Katie Barrett, Rosie Hackett, Máire Ryan, Bridget Davis, Chris Caffrey, P. Hoey, Miss Smith, Nora Foley, Pauline Morecambe, Dolly O'Sullivan, M. Elliot, Mollie O'Sullivan. T. Simpson, Catherine Treston, Nora Thornton, Rose Mullally, Sheila O'Hanlon, Maria Quigley, Margaret O'Flaherty, Josephine McGeown, E. (Lily) Cooney, Josephine O'Keeffe, May Moore, Kathleen Lane, Sara Kealy, G. Colley, M. O'Hanrahan, A. Wisely, Bridget Murtagh, S. Quigley, Julia Grenan, S. Twomey, B. Walsh, Rose MacNamara, Kathleen Kenny, Mary Joe Walsh, Mrs Lawless, J. Milner, Eileen Walsh, K. Kennedy, May Byrne, Annie Cooney, Madeleine ffrench-Mullen, Brigid Foley, Dr Kathleen Lynn.

Group of Limerick City Volunteers and Cumann na mBan. Front row, left to right: Mrs Bermingham, Mrs G. Clancy, Miss Downey, Mrs MacCormack, Mrs Crowe, Eileen O'Donoghue, Siún O'Farrell, Madge Daly, Carrie Daly. Captain Robert Monteith is on the far right of the back row.

Members of
Cumann na mBan.

Dr Kathleen Lynn

Annie Higgins

Winifred Carney

Madeleine ffrench-Mullen   Éilis Ní Rian (later Mrs Sean O'Connell)

Áine Ceannt

Countess Plunkett

Grace Gifford

Louise Gavan Duffy

Alice Stopford Green   Jenny Wyse Power

Julia Grenan   Rosanna (Rosie) Hackett

Hanna Sheehy-Skeffington

Lily O'Brennan

Maeve Cavanagh

Helena Molony

Una and Robert Brennan on their wedding day

Nora Connolly
(above) and in
Volunteers'
uniform *(left)*

Margaret Skinnider,
dressed as a boy *(above)*
and in her famous hat *(below)*

Sisters Peg and
Kattie Barrett
members of
Cumman na
mBan in Clare

Éilis Ní Chorra

Maud Gonne MacBride

Mary Spring-Rice

Mary MacSwiney

Constance Markievicz
at Thomas Ashe's funeral

Annie MacSwiney on hunger strke outside Mountjoy Prison, accompanied by Maud Gonne MacBride and others.
Mary MacSwiney was a prisoner on hunger strike inside the prison at the time.

Elizabeth O'Farrell

Máire Nic
Shiúbhlaigh,
a portrait by
John Butler Yeats

At the
Grosvenor Hotel,
London at the time of
meetings between
British
Prime Minister
Lloyd George and
President de Valera,
July 1921.

Left to right:
Count Plunkett, TD;
Erskine Childers, TD;
Laurence O'Neill,
Lord Mayor of
Dublin;
Lily O'Brennan;
Dr R Farnan;
Mrs Farnan;
Robert Barton, TD;
Kathleen O'Connell.
Seated:
Eamon de Valera,
Arthur Griffiths.

Women Volunteers
during the Civil War

He offered to have her driven home, but O'Farrell stated that she preferred to walk. She was then allowed to leave the Castle.

The last to surrender were the Enniscorthy insurgents. On Saturday, some women had left Enniscorthy on a scouting mission to Wexford. They returned with news of the arrival of British forces in the town. Later the Volunteer leaders were approached by a deputation including a priest and some local businessmen, who asked them to surrender in light of the situation in Dublin. It was eventually agreed that Enniscorthy Second Lieutenant, Seumas Ó Dubhghaill, would be given a safe conduct to go to see Pearse and receive the surrender order from him. On their return to Enniscorthy, the surrender was read to the Volunteers and Cumann na mBan on Monday afternoon. The republicans were later taken to Waterford jail.

When the Galway insurgents discussed whether to continue fighting or disband, the overwhelming majority decided they would continue to fight. Cumann na mBan members were strongly in favour of continuing. By Friday news of the deteriorating situation in Dublin reached them and in the early hours of Saturday it was decided — against Mellowes' advice — that the unit should disband. Mellowes and some of the other officers went on the run and about 100 Volunteers were subsequently arrested.

7
Prisoners

At Richmond Barracks, Julia Grenan and Winifred Carney were taken to a guardroom and then to the married quarters where they met other members of Cumann na mBan from the Four Courts. They saw Madeleine ffrench-Mullen and Constance Markievicz briefly. Markievicz ran over to speak to them but an officer ordered that she be taken away. She was held in solitary confinement and none of the other women saw her again until after her release. More than 3,000 prisoners passed through Richmond Barracks as a direct result of the Rising. Seventy-seven of them were women.

For the first few weeks the women were kept in Kilmainham. Dr Lynn and Helena Molony were among the women held there and Molony made an attempt to tunnel out using an iron spoon. She succeeded in dislodging two bricks and some plaster.

Four women were locked up to a cell, sharing two hard soldier's biscuits' beds and three dirty blankets between them. Meals consisted of cocoa and dry bread for breakfast; soup, beef, potatoes, cheese and bread for dinner; and 'skilly' for supper. Winifred Carney, Julia Grenan and Nell Gifford were put into the same cell. They were not given cutlery at Kilmainham, presumably because of Molony's escape attempts. 'So we had to keep some of the biscuits for the purpose of taking up the meat etc. and as they were not suitable for anything else, except perhaps doorstops, they stood the wear and tear admirably.'[1] Efforts to break these biscuits proved fruitless. Grenan kept her cellmates entertained — or distracted — with accounts of her favourite dishes. They sang songs such as 'Wrap the Green Flag' to keep their spirits up and all were prolific letter writers and letter smugglers. While in Kilmainham, Winifred Carney managed to smuggle out a letter from Joseph Plunkett to Grace Gifford.

Whenever the women left their cells, they had to run a gauntlet of jeering and abusive soldiers. The women ignored them 'and during their scant term of exercise danced Irish dances with as much appearance of carefree delight as if they were at some kindly ceilidh of the old days, instead of prisoners in the grip of the British Empire'.[2] Irish dancing was soon banned by the authorities and the women were confined to their cells if they attempted to defy the ban.

The women were deeply affected by the executions of the leaders of the Rising. These men had been close comrades and friends. When the executions began, the women could hear the shooting clearly from their cells, as Winifred Carney recalled.

> In the early morning of 3 May, I am awakened by the sound of firing and, in the after stillness, a low clear voice gives the order to quick march. They must be below our cell window ... My heart sinks, for I know the first of the executions has begun ... But for many mornings to come we shall awake to that close noise of rifle firing and the crisp voice of the officer in command.[3]

Min Ryan and her sister Phyllis were able to see Seán MacDiarmada the night before his execution.

On Monday 1 May, Marie Perolz, who until then had escaped arrest, saw prisoners including William Partridge, Kathleen Lynn and Helena Molony being marched under escort through the streets. About an hour later she herself was arrested. Others were also being rounded up; Kathleen Clarke was arrested with Arthur Griffith. Around midnight the military came for Kathleen. 'I suppose they are going to shoot Tom,'[4] she said to her friends and left the cell quietly.

Joseph Plunkett was responsible for much of the military strategy of the Rising, but had spent most of Easter week lying on a mattress in the GPO. He had suffered for many years from glandular tuberculosis, and was probably dying from it. He had recently had an operation on his throat and had taken himself out of hospital to participate in the Rising.

Plunkett and the artist Grace Gifford were to have been married that Easter, but their wedding had been postponed because of Joseph's illness and plans for the Rising. Knowing that Joseph would shortly be executed, they managed to obtain permission for their marriage in prison.

At about 5 p.m. on 3 May, Grace Gifford arrived by taxi at a jewellery shop in Grafton Street just as it was closing. She asked to buy a wedding ring. She then went straight to Kilmainham, where she was kept waiting until about 11.30 p.m. without being allowed to see Joseph. At last she was sent for. At 1.30 a.m. she was led into the prison chapel. Joseph was brought in in handcuffs. The electricity then failed and the ceremony took place by the light of a single candle, held by a British soldier. Twenty other soldiers, with bayonets fixed, lined the walls of the chapel.

The couple were separated immediately after the ceremony. Grace was allowed to see Joseph for 10 minutes shortly before dawn; 15 soldiers were crammed into the cell, one timing her visit with a watch. Joseph was executed at dawn. The following day, The *Irish Times* carried a brief marriage notice:

> PLUNKETT and GIFFORD, May 3, 1916 at Dublin, Joseph Plunkett and Grace Gifford.

Most of the women were released by 9 May. Five were deported to England and interned in Aylesbury prison. In July, two of the five, Brigid Foley and Marie Perolz, were released after appearing before a military court. Nell Ryan, Helena Molony and Winifred Carney were interned until December. Court appearances each lasted about three minutes. Efforts were made to get them to repudiate the Rising. Helena Molony responded that so far as the Irish Citizen Army was concerned, they had organised the Rising and would do so again.

Constance Markievicz was sentenced to death, but on the grounds that she was a woman the sentence was swiftly commuted to life imprisonment. She was held in Aylesbury apart from her friends where conditions were very hard. In an unusual appeal, the remaining three internees asked to be treated as convicts in order to be with Markiévicz. This was a particularly poignant act of friendship; the women had fought to force Britain to recognise their political rights and yet they were now prepared to forego all the benefits that were available to them as political internees and even agree to abide by the prison rules voluntarily. But uniquely, in this instance, the British government was not prepared to categorise Irish political prisoners as criminals.

> During the early autumn the Irish prisoners had made what must have seemed a quixotic request to the Home Office, a formal, written appeal to be allowed to live as convicts in the convict wing with Countess Markievicz. They agreed to give up all their privileges, letters, visits, food, other than those allowed to the long-term convicts ... They further pledged themselves not to use their prison grievances as propaganda in the future and not to communicate further in any illicit manner with the outside world. The latter they considered was a major concession. It was notorious that since the coming of "the three Irish" to Aylesbury, a constant flow of news and messages got out to the press and to the families and friends of the unfortunate women who were spies or suspected of being spies — German, Greek, Belgian, English. Their request was "disallowed" by the Home Office and the prisoners withdrew their offer.[5]

The conditions in the section of the prison reserved for convicted prisoners were very bad and Markievicz's experiences there inspired her to campaign against prison conditions for the rest of her life. Even under these oppressive circumstances, she managed to concern herself with the welfare of others. She wrote to her sister Eva Gore-Booth to arrange for a weekly payment to Bessie Lynch, who had been working for her at her home, Surrey House. She also arranged for Bridie Gough to receive at least a month's wages. Bridie had also been employed by Markievicz and had been arrested with her. Constance Markievicz was finally released in June 1917. Helena Molony and Marie Perolz travelled to England to meet her on her release.

Most of the male prisoners were held in England. Two hundred were taken to Barlinnie in August but were moved because of the support they received from the Irish community in Glasgow and from the Scottish suffragettes who organised regular visits and took parcels to the prisoners.

Epilogue

> We failed, but not until we had seen regiment after regiment
> run from our few guns. Our effort will inspire the people
> who come after us, and will give them hope and courage. If
> we failed to win, so did the English. They slaughtered and
> imprisoned, only to arouse the nation to a passion of love
> and loyalty, loyalty to Ireland and hatred of foreign rule.
> Once they see clearly that the English rule us still, only with
> a new personnel of traitors and new uniforms, they will
> finish the work begun by the men and women of Easter
> Week.[1]

After the rising, any sort of republican political activity was
very difficult, but the women started immediately to organise
on behalf of the prisoners and to provide for the dependents of
prisoners and of those who had died. Cumann na mBan had
£200 in hand, which was used to alleviate hardship until the
Irish National Aid Association's Fund was established. This
fund provided help to families and also paid for food and
clothing parcels which were sent into the prisons. It was not
long, also, before Cumann na mBan began to collect funds for
the re-equipping and rearming of the Volunteers.

The work the women did at this time was motivated by more
than humanitarian concerns. While the support given to
prisoners and their families was absolutely vital to the well-
being of the individual people involved, the political
significance of this work was immense.

> It was around efforts on behalf of the prisoners and the
> dependants of the killed and wounded of Easter Week that
> the new Sinn Fein movement was organised in Ireland.

Within a few days of the execution of Thomas Clarke his
widow had begun to gather together the broken threads. An
Irish National Aid Association and an Irish Volunteer
Dependants' Fund were formed. Groups that might otherwise
have scattered, forces that might have disintegrated, were
held together by this appeal, and the young men and women
who were coming forward to take part in the Republican
struggle were enlisted in this work.[2]

The Officers of the Irish Volunteer Dependants' Fund were
Kathleen Clarke, President; Áine Ceannt, Vice-President;
S. Nic Mhathghamha, Treasurer; E. MacRaghnaill, Secretary;
Mrs Pearse; Muriel McDonagh; Eily O'Hanrahan, Madge Daly
and Lila Colbert. The Irish Volunteer Dependants' Fund
subsequently amalgamated with the Irish National Aid
Association.

In the autumn of 1916, despite the severe repression of
nationalist organisations, Cumann na mBan was able to hold a
convention. At its convention in 1917, 200 branches were
represented. The organisation passed a resolution calling for
'the realisation of the Declaration embodied in the Proclamation
of 1916 guaranteeing equal rights and liberties for all ... by
educating the people of Ireland in, and urging them to adopt a
social policy as outlined by James Connolly.'[3]

Min Ryan was sent by Cumann na mBan as its first envoy to
the United States, to tell the story of the rising and to raise
funds for relief work. Nora Connolly and Hanna Sheehy-
Skeffington also went to America — both without passports —
to speak about the rising.

When Liam Mellowes was arrested in New York in 1917,
Nora Connolly and Margaret Skinnider had the job of retrieving
papers he had left hidden. Nora Connolly had some difficulty
in getting back into Ireland. Eventually she managed to cross
from Liverpool disguised as a boy.

The Sinn Féin executive was reorganised in October 1917. It
included among its 24 members Kathleen Clarke, Kathleen
Lynn, Grace Plunkett and Constance Markievicz.

In 1918, women were active in the anti-conscription
campaign. The Irish Women Workers' Union marched its

members through Dublin during a 24-hour strike against plans for conscription. Cumann na mBan organised an 'All-Ireland Women's Day' against conscription.

Hanna Sheehy-Skeffington was arrested and imprisoned with Kathleen Clarke in Holloway in 1918. Their fellow prisoners were Constance Markievicz and Maud Gonne. In the December elections in 1918, Markievicz was elected as the first woman MP while a prisoner in Holloway jail.

The First Dáil took an historic stance — unique among the nations of the western world — in its 1919 Programme which declared:

> We affirm the duty of every man and woman to give allegiance and service to the commonwealth, and declare it the duty of the nation to assure that every citizen shall have opportunity to spend his or her strength and faculties in the service of the people. In return for willing service, we, in the name of the Republic, declare the right of every citizen to an adequate share of the produce of the nation's labour.[4]

Constance Markievicz was the Minister of Labour.

Markievicz was later to explain, in a debate in the Dáil in 1921, how her political commitment to equality had developed. Recalling her early involvement in the Sligo Women's Suffrage Society, she said:

> It is one of the things that I have worked for since I was a young girl. That was my first bite, you may say, at the apple of freedom and soon I got on to the other freedoms, freedom to the nation, freedom to the workers. The question of votes for women, with the bigger thing, freedom for women and the opening of the professions to women, has been one of the things that I have worked for and given my influence and time to procuring all my life whenever I got an opportunity. I have worked in Ireland, I have even worked in England, to help women to obtain their freedom. I would work for it anywhere, as one of the crying wrongs of the world, that women, because of their sex, should be debarred from any position or any right that their brains entitle them to hold.[5]

Kathleen Lynn, who was highly respected in Dublin medical circles, became a popular hero for her outstanding work during the great influenza epidemic that raged through Dublin in 1918. Nevertheless, her surgery was frequently raided and she was arrested and held for deportation at the height of the epidemic. This provoked such a public outcry that she was released and the Lord Mayor of Dublin offered an armed guard for her protection.

Even before the War of Independence began in 1919, women were again to the fore in military preparations. Linda Kearns wrote: "Those of us who gave our all in '16 were not likely to be backward when the call came for our services again."[6]

In July 1920, republican courts of justice were set up to replace the British judicial system. The justices were men and women elected by the Sinn Féin clubs, persons without special legal training, but whose judgement and fairness could be relied upon. Maud Gonne McBride and Kathleen Clarke were among the justices. When a woman was being tried there was usually a woman on the bench. The courts operated in 27 of Ireland's 32 counties.

In November 1920, Linda Kearns was arrested in Sligo while driving a car carrying three IRA Volunteers; they had with them 10 rifles and 500 rounds of ammunition. The arresting patrol included British soldiers, RIC men and Black and Tans. She was held overnight and badly beaten by the Auxiliaries when she refused to give them information. They struck her in the face, breaking several of her teeth and threatening to kill her. In April 1921, she was sentenced in a Belfast court to 10 years in prison. She later escaped from Mountjoy jail with Eithne Coyle, May Burke and Eileen Keogh. She continued on active service until 1923.

Linda Kearns, who later became a Free State Senator under de Valera, was awarded the Florence Nightingale medal from the International Red Cross on her deathbed. She died in the rest and holiday home for nurses she had helped to found. For over 35 years she had devoted herself to the causes of Irish independence and better living and working conditions for nurses.

During the Civil War, women played a major role, on both sides, but particularly as part of the anti-Treaty forces. Women were inside the Four Courts until the surrender and there were three women under Cathal Brugha's command when he was killed. Cumann na mBan organised a big public funeral for Brugha at a time when it was impossible for male republicans to march in Dublin city.

The bravery of the republican women was exemplified by an incident in which Molly Hyland, a Cumann na mBan officer, had to bring into Dublin the body of an IRA Volunteer killed in a fight in the Dublin mountains. She had to prop him up in the passenger seat of the car, as if he were still alive, to avoid being arrested.

For the first time in modern Irish history, the Civil War brought mass imprisonment of women. Many republican women were held in the North Dublin Union and forced to sleep outside. About 30 of these prisoners, including Máire Comerford, managed to escape, but with only one exception were recaptured. The women being held in Kilmainham were to be transferred to North Dublin Union. Mary MacSwiney and Catherine O'Callaghan were on hunger strike and the other prisoners refused to leave them. Late at night soldiers were sent in to remove them by force. Fighting went on all night and prisoners were dragged down the iron staircases from landing to landing. Finally about two-thirds of the battered prisoners were removed. In Mountjoy, Máire Comerford was shot in the leg after waving at other prisoners on exercise. Towards the end of the struggle, women in North Dublin Union went on mass hunger strike. The hunger strike lasted 31 days.

The Irish White Cross was formed at the end of 1920 to provide relief for families in distress as a result of the War of Independence. After 1922 it became known as the Children's Relief Association and extended its assistance to children whose parents — on both sides of the fight — had been killed or incapacitated as a result of the Civil War. Kathleen Clarke, Madame O'Rahilly, Maud Gonne McBride, Kathleen Lynn and

Máire Comerford remained on the board of the Association until its winding up in 1936. The Association took an active interest in the fortunes of the children it assisted, requiring them to attend school regularly until they were of age and then providing a lump sum at the age of 16 which could be used for apprenticeship fees, vocational training, university fees or to start up in business.

> Easter Week and its aftermath of blood and tears passed, and no doubt England in her stupidity believed that she had quenched the sparks of rebellion beyond rekindling. All the world knows now that the contrary was the result, and that from the smouldering embers of that week flared up the mighty blaze that was to light our land from end to end.[7]

After the dissolution of the Ladies' Land League, women had to reorganise and insist upon their right to active participation in public and political life. The nationalist revival of the late 19th and early 20th centuries brought together women like Jenny Wyse Power, who had been active in the Ladies' Land League, and a new generation of young women. These women in turn fought for their place in the revived nationalist movement, participated in the emerging labour movement and won votes for women. They fought in the Easter Rising of 1916, the War of Independence and the Civil War. Women — in some cases these same individuals — served terms in prison and in the Oireachtas. After the Civil War the most socially and politically progressive sections of Irish society were fragmented and demoralised. Those who were not imprisoned often found themselves without employment and forced to emigrate. Ireland became conservative and inward-looking. The Celtic Renaissance was replaced with gombeen men. The 1935 Conditions of Employment Bill and De Valera's Constitution of 1937 gave legal imprimatur to the renewed exclusion of women from employment opportunities and public life. The 1937 Constitution represented the defeat of those women and their male allies who had worked so hard over the previous six decades, linking the struggle for equality between men and women with the struggles for national freedom and democracy.

It is time to resurrect the stories of all those women who were pushed to the margins in the 1930s, '40s, '50s and '60s and rediscover those women who have provided the living links with the women of the 1970s, '80s and '90s, who are struggling once again to achieve a synthesis between feminism and nationalism.

, p. 150
2. *Ibid*, p. 151.
3. *Ibid*, p. 96.
4. *Ibid*, p. 168.
5. *Ibid*, p. 52.

Chapter 1: Women Organising

1. R. M. Fox, *Green Banners*, p. 57.
2. Gifford Lewis, *Eva Gore-Booth and Esther Roper: a Biography*, p. 105.
3. James Connolly, *Irish Worker*, 28 November 1914.
4. Jacqueline Van Voris, *Constance Markievicz: in the Cause of Ireland*, p. 132.
5. Louise Gavan Duffy, "In the G.P.O.: Cumann na mBan", Translation by J. Jackson. Published as Lúise Ghabhánach Ní Dhubhthaigh, "Insan G.P.O.: Cumann na mBan".
6. Robert Brennan, *Allegiance*, p. 11.
7. Éilis Ní Chorra, "A Rebel Remembers", p. 292.
8. *Ibid.*, p. 292.
9. *Ibid.*, p. 294.
10. *Ibid.*, p. 295.
11. Margaret Skinnider, *Doing My Bit for Ireland*, p. 6.
12. Kathleen Keyes McDonnell, *There is a Bridge at Bandon: A Personal Account of the Irish War of Independence*, p. 30.
13. *Ibid.*, p. 31.
14. *Ibid.*, p. 32.
15. Mannix Joyce, "The Story of Limerick and Kerry", p. 332.

Chapter 2: Military and Political Preparations

1. Mary Spring-Rice, "Excerpts from the Diary on the 'Asgard'", *Sinn Féin*, 26 July 1924.
2. Mary Spring-Rice, *Ibid.*, 2 August, 1924.
3. *Ibid.*
4. *Ibid.*
5. Nora Connolly O'Brien, *Portrait of a Rebel Father*, quoted in Van Voris, p. 137.
6. *Ibid.*
7. R. M. Fox, *History of the Irish Citizen Army*, p. 112.
8. *Ibid.*, p. 113.
9. Helena Molony, *Years of Tension*.

10. Matt Connolly, "Dublin City Hall Area", p. 194.
11. Nora O'Daly, "The Women of Easter Week".
12. Margaret Skinnider, *Doing My Bit,* pp. 9-10.
13. *Ibid.,* pp. 50-51.
14. *Ibid.,* p. 42.
15. Nora O'Daly, *op. cit.*
16. Frank Robbins, *Under the Starry Plough: Recollections of the Irish Citizen Army,* p. 160.
17. John Devoy, *Recollections of an Irish Rebel,* p. 460.
18. R. M. Fox, *How the Women Helped,* pp. 209.
19. R. M. Fox, *History of the Irish Citizen Army,* p. 133.
20. Margaret Skinnider, *op. cit.,* p. 69.
21. Helena Molony, *op. cit.*
22. Leslie Bean de Barra, interview in Donncha Ó Dúlaing, *Voices of Ireland,* pp. 93-94.
23. Kathleen Clarke, *Revolutionary Woman: Kathleen Clarke 1878-1972. An Autobiography,* p. 68.
24. Leslie Bean de Barra, *op. cit.,* p. 94.
25. Julia Grenan, interview in Donncha Ó Dúlaing, *op. cit.,* p. 70.
26. R. M. Fox, *Green Banners,* p. 191.
27. R. M. Fox, "The Irish Citizen Army," in *Eirí Amach na Cásca,* p. 25.
28. Margaret Skinnider, *Irish Press,* 9 March 1966.
29. Margaret Skinnider, *Doing My Bit for Ireland,* p. 79.
30. Kathleen Keyes McDonnell, *op. cit.,* p. 44.
31. *Ibid.,* p. 45.
32. *Ibid.,* p. 47.

Chapter 3: Mobilisation and Countermand

1. Nora Connolly O'Brien, interview in Donncha Ó Dúlaing, *op. cit.,* p. 81.
2. Nora Connolly O'Brien, *We Shall Rise Again,* p. 31.
3. Betsy Gray, "A Memory of Easter Week," p. 282.
4. R. M. Fox, *Green Banners,* p. 243.
5. Lily O'Brennan, "The Dawning of the Day", p. 158.
6. *Ibid.,* p. 158.
7. *Ibid.,* p. 158.
8. Nora O'Daly, *op. cit.*
9. Florence O'Donoghue, *Tómas MacCurtain, Soldier and Patriot: A Biography of the First Republican Lord Mayor of Cork,* p. 105.
10. Julia Grenan, *op. cit.,* p. 70.
11. Seumas Ó Dubhghaill, "When Wexford Rose".
12. Elizabeth O'Farrell, "Recollections", 26 April, 1930.
13. *Ibid.*

Chapter 4: Dublin Fights

1. R. M. Fox, "The Irish Citizen Army", p. 26.
2. Leslie de Barra, in Donncha Ó Dúlaing, *op. cit.*, p. 96.
3. Louise Gavan Duffy, *op. cit.*
4. *Ibid.*
5. Constance Markievicz, "Women in the Fight", p. 123.
6. Matt Connolly, *op. cit.*, p. 198.
7. *Ibid.*, p. 200.
8. *Ibid.*, p. 200.
9. R. M. Fox, *Green Banners*, p. 153.
10. *Ibid.*, p. 153.
11. Margaret Skinnider, *Doing My Bit for Ireland*, p. 167.
12. Constance Markievicz, "Women in the Fight", p. 123.
13. Frank Robbins, *op. cit.*, p. 131.
14. Margaret Skinnider, *op. cit.*, p. 95.
15. *Ibid.*, p. 122-124.
16. Cmdt Andy McDonnell, interview, *Irish Press*, April 1964, quoted in Roger McHugh, p. 178.
17. Cmdt Joseph O'Connor, "Boland's Mills Area", p. 242.
18. George A. Lyons, "Recollections".
19. Lily O'Brennan, *op. cit.*, p. 159.
20. *Ibid.*, p. 159.
21. A Volunteer, "South Dublin Union Area", p. 208.
22. Mary Donnelly, *The Last Post Glasnevin Cemetery: being a record of Ireland's Heroic Dead in Dublin City and County and Places of Historic Interest*, p. 26.
23. R. M. Fox, "How the Women Helped", p. 209.
24. Máire Nic Shiubhlaigh, *The Splendid Years*, p. 165.
25. *Ibid.*, p. 174.
26. Frank Robbins, *op. cit.*, pp. 94-95.
27. *Sinn Féin Rebellion Handbook*, p. 19.
28. Constance Markievicz, *op. cit.*, p. 123.
29. Mary Donnelly, "With the Citizen Army in Stephen's Green".
30. Constance Markievicz, *op. cit.*, p. 124.
31. Liam Ó Briain, "Saint Stephen's Green Area", p. 233.
32. A Red Cross Nurse, "The Dublin Forts", p. 143.
33. R. M. Fox, *Green Banners*, p. 293.
34. Julia Grenan, *Recollections*, 17 May 1930.
35. Julia Grenan, in Ó Dúlaing, *op. cit.*, p. 71.
36. *Ibid.*
37. R. M. Fox, *Green Banners*, pp. 294-295.
38. Julia Grenan, in Ó Dúlaing, *op. cit.*, p. 73.
39. Frank Robbins, *op. cit.*, p. 118.
40. R. M. Fox, *History of the Irish Citizen Army*, p. 163.
41. Commandant W. J. Brennan-Whitmore, "The Occupation of the North Earl Street Area".
42. A Red Cross Nurse, *op. cit.*, p. 143.

43. Margaret Skinnider, *Doing My Bit for Ireland*, p. 143.
44. Nora Connolly O'Brien, in Ó Dúlaing, *op. cit.*, p. 80.
45. Liam Ó Briain, *op. cit.*, p. 233.
46. Constance Markievicz, *op. cit.*, p. 125.

Chapter 5: A City on Fire

1. "A Record by Rev. John Flanagan, C.C.," in McHugh, *op. cit.*, p. 191.
2. Leslie de Barra, in Ó Dúlaing, *op. cit.*, p. 97.
3. *Ibid.*, pp. 97-98.
4. Commandant W. J. Brennan-Whitmore, *op. cit.*
5. *Ibid.*
6. *Ibid.*
7. Annie Higgins, letter to Gertrude Gaffney, quoted in Gertrude Gaffney, "Annie Higgins".
8. Seumas Ó Dubhghaill, "When Wexford Rose".
9. Nora Connolly O'Brien, in Ó Dúlaing, *op. cit.*, p. 81.
10. Betsy Gray, *op. cit.*, p. 284.
11. Nora Connolly O'Brien, in Ó Dúlaing, *op. cit.*, p. 82.
12. *Ibid.*, p. 84.
13. Eoin Ó Brien, (ed.) *The Charitable Infirmary...*, p. 38.
14. *ibid.*
15. *ibid.*
16. *ibid.*
17. Leslie de Barra, *op. cit.*, pp. 100-101.
18. Louise Gavan Duffy, *op. cit.*
19. *Ibid.*
20. Leslie de Barra, *op. cit.*, p. 97.
21. Elizabeth O'Farrell, *Catholic Bulletin*, April 1917, p. 266.
22. Linda Kearns, *In Times of Peril*, p. 8.

Chapter 6: Saturday - The Surrender

1. Elizabeth O'Farrell, *Catholic Bulletin*, April 1917, p. 267.
2. Julia Grenan, *Catholic Bulletin*, June 1917, p. 396.
3. *Ibid.*, p. 396.
4. A Member of Cumann na mBan, *Gaelic American*, 18 November 1916.
5. Elizabeth O'Farrell, *Catholic Bulletin*, p. 268.
6. Julia Grenan, in Ó Dúlaing, *op. cit.*, p. 75.
7. Éilis Bean Uí Chonaill, "A Cumann na mBan Recalls Easter Week", p. 276.
8. *Ibid.*, p. 276.
9. *Ibid.* p. 276
10. R. M. Fox, *Green Banners*, p. 291.
11. A Cumann na mBan Member, *Gaelic American*, 11 November 1916.
12. Liam Ó Briain, *op. cit.*, p. 236.
13. Frank Robbins, *op. cit.*, p. 127.

14. *Sinn Féin Rebel Handbook*, p. 19.
15. Elizabeth Coxhead, *op. cit.*, p. 157.
16. Nora O'Daly, *op. cit.*
17. Elizabeth O'Farrell, *Catholic Bulletin*, May 1917, p. 329.
18. *Ibid.*, p. 330.
19. *Ibid.*, p. 330.
20. *Ibid.*, p. 331.
21. Máire nic Shuibhlaigh, *op. cit.*, p. 184.
22. Louise Gavan Duffy, *op. cit.*
23. Mary Donnelly, *op. cit.*
24. Kenneth Griffith and Timothy E. O'Grady, *Curious Journey: An Oral History of Ireland's Unfinished Revolution*, p. 74.
25. *Ibid.*, p. 75.
26. *Ibid.*, p. 77.
27. *Ibid.*, p. 78.
28. Elizabeth O'Farrell, *Catholic Bulletin*, May 1917, p. 332.
29. *Ibid.*, p. 333.

Chapter 7: Prisoners

1. Nora O'Daly, *op. cit.*
2. "Dublin Castle from the Inside", *An t-Oglach*, 13 February 1926.
3. R. M. Fox, *Green Banners*, p. 292.
4. R. M. Fox, *History of the Irish Citizen Army*, p. 184.
5. Jacqueline Van Voris, *op. cit.*, p. 221.

Epilogue

1. Constance Markievicz, *op. cit.*, p. 125.
2. Dorothy Macardle, *The Irish Republic*, p. 208.
3. R. M. Fox, *How the Women Helped*, p. 211.
4. Programme of the First Dáil, quoted in Dorothy Macardle, *op. cit.*, p. 287.
5. Jacqueline Van Voris, *op. cit.*, p. 309.
6. Linda Kearns, *op. cit.*, p.8.
7. *Ibid.*, p. 8.

Bibliography

Aloysis, Fr., O.F.M. Cap., "Personal Recollections", *The Capuchin Annual*, 1966.

Birtill, Tony, "Connolly Back in Liverpool," *Irish Post*, London, 16 April 1988.

Brennan, Robert, *Allegiance*, Browne and Nolan Limited, Dublin, 1950.

Brennan-Whitmore, Commandant W. J., "The Occupation of the North Earl Street Area", *An t-Oglach*, 30 January and 6 February, 1926.

Bean Uí Chonail, Éilis, "A Cumann na mBan Recalls Easter Week", *The Capuchin Annual*, 1966.

Clarke, Kathleen, *Revolutionary Woman: Kathleen Clarke 1878-1972. An Autobiography*, edited by Helen Litton, O'Brien Press, Dublin, 1991.

Conlon, Lil, *Cumann na mBan and the Women of Ireland 1913-1972*, Kilkenny People, Kilkenny, 1969.

Comerford, Máire, "Women in Struggle", *Eiri Amach na Casca*, edited by Pat McGlynn, Republican Publications, Dublin, 1986.

Comerford, Máire, *Irish Press*, 9 April 1966.

Connolly, Matt, "Dublin City Hall Area", *The Capuchin Annual*, 1966.

Cooney, Annie, "The Marrowbone Lane Post", *An Phoblacht*, 26 May 1930.

Coyle, Eithne, "The History of Cumann na mBan", *An Phoblacht*, 8 April 1933.

Coxhead, Elizabeth, *Daughters of Erin: Five Women of the Irish Renaissance*, Colin Smythe, Gerrards Cross, 1979.

Cullen Owens, Rosemary, *Smashing Times: A History of the Irish Women's Suffrage Movement 1889-1922*, Attic Press, Dublin, 1984.

Daly, James, Sen., "General Post Office Area", *The Capuchin Annual*, 1966.

Devoy, John, *Recollections of an Irish Rebel*, Irish University Press, Shannon, 1969; first published 1929.

Donnelly, Mary, *The Last Post Glasnevin Cemetery: Being a Record of Ireland's Heroic Dead in Dublin City and County, Also Places of Historic Interest*, National Graves Association, Dublin, first published 1932.

Donnelly, Mary, "With the Citizen Army in Stephen's Green", *An Phoblacht*, 19 April 1930.

"Dublin Castle from the Inside", *An t-Oglach*, 13 February 1926.

"Events of Easter Week", *Catholic Bulletin*, 1916-1918 (including accounts by Elizabeth O'Farrell and Julia Grenan).

Fallon, Charlotte H., *Soul of Fire: A Biography of Mary MacSwiney*, Mercier Press, Dublin, 1986.

Fox, R. M., *Rebel Irishwomen*, Progress House, Dublin, 1935.

Fox, R. M., *Green Banners: The Story of the Irish Struggle*, Secker and Warburg, London, 1938.

Fox, R. M., *The History of the Irish Citizen Army*, James Duffy, Dublin, 1943.

Fox, R. M., "How the Women Helped", in *Dublin's Fighting Story*, 1916-21, The Kerryman, Tralee.

Gaffney, Gertrude, "Annie Higgins", *The Capuchin Annual*, 1936.

Gavan Duffy, Louise, "In the G.P.O.: Cumann na mBan", in F.X. Martin (ed.) *The Easter Rising 1916*, Browne and Nolan, Dublin, 1966. Translation by J. Jackson. (Published as Lúise Ghabhánach Ní Dhubhthaigh, "Insan G.P.O.: Cumann na mBan".)

Gifford, Lewis, *Eva Gore Booth and Esther Roper: A Biography*, Pandora, London, 1988.

Gray, Betsy, "A Memory of Easter Week," *The Capuchin Annual*, 1948.

Greaves, Desmond, *Liam Mellowes and the Irish Revolution*, Lawrence and Wishart, London, 1971.

Greaves, Desmond, *The Life and Times of James Connolly*, Lawrence and Wishart, London, 1976.

Griffith, Kenneth and Timothy E. O'Grady, *Curious Journey: An Oral History of Ireland's Unfinished Revolution*, Hutchinson, London, 1982.

Haverty, Ann, *Constance Markievicz: An Independent Life*, Pandora, London, 1988.

Joyce, Mannix, "The Story of Limerick and Kerry in 1916", *The Capuchin Annual*, 1966.

Kearns, Linda, *In Times of Peril*, Talbot Press, Dublin, 1922.

Lawless, Joseph, Captain, "The Fight at Ashbourne", *An t-Oglach*, 31 July 1926.

Lawless, Joseph, Colonel, "The Fight at Ashbourne", *The Capuchin Annual*, 1966.

Lyons, George A., "Recollections", *An t-Oglach*, 10 April 1926.

Lyons, J. B., *Brief Lives of Irish Doctors*, Blackwater Press, Dublin, 1978.

Macardle, Dorothy, *The Irish Republic*, Farrar, Strauss and Giroux, New York, 1937; reprinted 1965.

McCann, John, *War by the Irish*, The Kerryman, Tralee, 1946.

MacCurtain, Margaret, "Women, The Vote and Revolution", in Margaret MacCurtain and Donncha Ó Corrain, (eds.), *Women in Irish Society: The Historical Dimension*, Arlen House, The Women's Press, Dublin, 1978.

McCullough, Denis, "The Events in Belfast", *The Capuchin Annual*, 1966.

McCullough, Denis, "What Happened in Ulster?" *Irish Independent 1916-'66 Supplement*, Dublin, 1966.

McDonnell, Kathleen Keyes, *There is a Bridge at Bandon: A Personal Account of the Irish War of Independence*, Mercier Press, Cork and Dublin, 1972.

McHugh, Roger, *Dublin 1916*, Arlington Books, Dublin, 1966.

Markievicz, Constance, "Women in the Fight", in Roger McHugh, *Dublin 1916*, Dublin, 1966.

Martin, F. X., O.S.A., general editor, *1916 and University College Dublin*, Browne and Nolan, Dublin, 1966.

Missing Pieces: Women in Irish History, Irish Feminist Information Publications, Dublin, 1983.

More Missing Pieces: Her Story of Irish History, Attic Press, Dublin, 1985.

Ní Chorra, Éilis, "A Rebel Remembers", *The Capuchin Annual*, 1936.

Nic Shiubhlaigh, Máire, *The Splendid Years*, James Duffy, Dublin, 1955.

Norman, Diana, *Terrible Beauty: A Life of Constance Markievicz*, Hodder and Stoughton, London, 1988.

Neilan, Mattie, "The Rising in Galway", *The Capuchin Annual*, 1966.

O'Brennan, Lily, "The Dawning of the Day", *The Capuchin Annual*, 1936.

Ó Briain, Liam, "Saint Stephen's Green Area", *The Capuchin Annual*, 1966.

O'Brien, Eoin (ed.) *The Charitable Infirmary Jervis Street 1718-1987: A Farewell Tribute*, Anniversary Press, Dublin, 1987.

O'Brien, Nora Connolly, *We Shall Rise Again*, Mosquito Press, London, 1981.

O'Brien, William and Desmond Ryan, *Devoy's Post Bag, Vol. II*, Academy Press, Dublin, reissued 1979.

Ó Ceallaigh, Padraig, "Jacob's Factory Area", *The Capuchin Annual*, 1966.

O'Connor, Joseph, Commandant, "Boland's Mills Area", *The Capuchin Annual*, 1966.

O'Daly, Nora, "The Women of Easter Week", *An t-Oglach*, 3 April, 1926.

O'Delany, Barry, "Cumann na mBan: The Women's Auxiliary of the Irish Army", in William G. Fitz-Gerald, (ed.), *Voice of Ireland*, John Heywood, Dublin, 1924.

O'Donoghue, Florence, *Tomás MacCurtain, Soldier and Patriot: A Biography of the First Republican Lord Mayor of Cork*, Anvil Press, Tralee, 1971.

Ó Dubhghaill, Séumas, "Activities in Enniscorthy", *The Capuchin Annual*, 1966.

Ó Dúbhghaill, Séumas, "When Wexford Rose", *Irish Independent 1916-'66 Supplement*, Dublin, 1966.

Ó Dúlaing, Donncha, *Voices of Ireland*, O'Brien Press, Dublin, 1984.

O'Farrell, Elizabeth, "Recollections", *An Phoblacht*, 26 April, 3 and 10 May 1930.

O'Neill, Charles, "At the Barricades in '16", *An Phoblacht*, 3 May 1930.

'A Red Cross Nurse', "The Dublin Forts" in Padraic Colum and others, *The Irish Rebellion of 1916 and Its Martyrs*, Maurice Joy, (ed.), New York, Devin-Adair, 1916.

Report of the Meeting of the Irish White Cross, Children's Relief Association (Incorporated) held on 1st September, 1936, Three Candles, Dublin, 1936.

Reynolds, M., "Cumann na mBan in the GPO", *An t-Oglach*, 27 March 1926.

Robbins, Frank, *Under the Starry Plough: Recollections of the Irish Citizen Army*, Academy Press, Dublin, 1977.

Ruiséal, Liam, "The Position in Cork", *The Capuchin Annual*, 1966.

Ryan, Desmond, *The Rising: The Complete Story of Easter Week,* Golden Eagle Books Ltd, Dublin, 1949.

Sheehy-Skeffington, Hanna, "Constance Markievicz in 1916", *An Phoblacht*, 14 April 1928.

Sinn Féin Rebellion Handbook: Easter 1916, compiled by the *Weekly Irish Times*, Fred Hanna, Dublin, 1917.

Skinnider, Margaret, *Doing My Bit for Ireland*, Century, New York, 1917.

Spring Rice, Mary, "Excerpts from the Diary on the 'Asgard'", *Sinn Féin*, 26 July and 2 August 1924.

Sweeney, P. Emmet, "Recollections of a Volunteer", *An t-Oglach*, 10 March 1930.

Turner, C., Captain, "The Defence of Hopkins & Hopkins, O'Connell Street, Dublin", *An t-Oglach*, 5 June 1926.

Turner, C., Captain, "The Kimmage Garrison", *An t-Oglach*, 1 May 1926.

Van Voris, Jacqueline, *Constance de Markievicz: in the Cause of Ireland*, University of Massachusetts Press, 1967.

'A Volunteer', "South Dublin Union Area", *The Capuchin Annual*, 1966.

Ward, Margaret, *Unmanageable Revolutionaries: Women and Irish Nationalism*, Pluto Press, London, 1983.

Wyse Power, Jenny, Senator, "The Political Influence of Women in Modern Ireland", in William G. Fitz-Gerald, (ed.), *The Voice of Ireland*, John Heywood, Dublin, 1924.

Young, Thomas, Captain, "With the Garrison in Marrowbone Lane During Easter Week", *An t-Oglach*, 6 March 1926.

Index